THERE'S NOTHING LIKE A
Testimony

Only believe!

SHAWANDA PAULDIN

Shawanda Pauldin

WONDROUS WORKS LLC

There's Nothing Like a Testimony
Copyright © 2014 by Shawanda Pauldin.

All rights reserved. No part of this publication may be reproduced in any form without the prior written permission of the publisher except for brief quotations in printed reviews.

Scripture quotations marked AMP are taken from the Amplified Bible, Copyright © 1954, 1958, 1962, 1964, 1965, 1987 by The Lockman Foundation. Used by permission.

Scripture quotations marked NLT are taken from the Holy Bible, New Living Translation, copyright © 1996, 2004, 2007 by Tyndale House Foundation. Used by permission of Tyndale House Publishers, Inc., Carol Stream, Illinois 60188. All rights reserved.

Scripture quotations marked TLB are taken from The Living Bible copyright © 1971. Used by permission of Tyndale House Publishers, Inc., Carol Stream, Illinois 60188. All rights reserved.

Scripture quotations marked NKJV are taken from the New King James Version®. Copyright © 1982 by Thomas Nelson, Inc. Used by permission. All rights reserved.

Scripture quotations marked The Message are taken from *THE MESSAGE*. Copyright © by Eugene H. Peterson 1993, 1994, 1995, 1996, 2000, 2001, 2002. Used by permission of NavPress Publishing Group. All rights reserved.

Wondrous Works LLC
P.O. Box 1092
Fayetteville, GA 30214

www.WWinspires.com

ISBN: 978-0-9913846-0-0

Author photo by Andre Doanes
Edited by With Pen In Hand
Cover design by Damonza
Interior design by Six Penny Graphics

Printed in the United States of America

Contents

Introduction 1

Hearing His Will 5
What's Your Motive? 7
Is That You, God? 9
Would Love Do That? 11
Baskets for Blessing 13
Share His Love 15
Rules of the World 17
Seed for the Sower 19
It Can Happen Just Like That! 21
I am a Creator 23
My Real Employer 24
The Thankfulness List 26
A Willing Heart 28
No Job…NO PROBLEM 30
I'm Healed and That's That 33
Right Place, Right Time 35

A Trip to the Airport 37

The Desires of My Heart 40

A Reservation for Four, Please 43

Everything is Lovely 45

Manifestation Time 46

He Showed Up With My Clothes 48

A Box of Blessings 50

That's the One 52

Don't Take That Shortcut 55

Follow the System 57

On the Auction Block 59

Unexpected Increase 61

My Best Effort 63

Signs and Symptoms—Not Facts 65

He Will Supply 67

It's All in My Mind 69

What Should I Do, God? 72

Rewards of Overcoming the Flesh 74

Do You Have the Guts? 76

Confession Means Protection 78

Acknowledge Him 80

He Knows Our Needs 82

Untapped Potential 84

That Doesn't Belong to Me 86

A 7-Day Diet 88

Something for Joshua 90

Merry Christmas! 92

Whatever	93
Thinking Outside the Box	97
Honor Breeds Honor	100
Out of the Mouth of Babes	103
A Few Butterflies, But Pressing On	105
Faithful Family Members	109
Do It Afraid	111
Act Like It's So	114
A True Christ-like One	116
Exceeding Abundantly Above	117
Scrumptious Strawberries	119
Yay! We Have Tenants!	121
Promotion in the House	122
The $50 Shoes	124
Unfinished and Underdeveloped	126
Slam on Brakes and Pray	128
I'm Only a Vessel	130
About the Author	131

Introduction

As a housewife, I was in the minority among my friends and associates in 1999. Many of them either disliked their jobs or were genuinely unhappy with the circumstances of their lives. For this reason, I began sending words of encouragement via email with hopes of brightening their days. "MEDITATION" was the subject line I used for each message. From 1999 through 2007, I forwarded these communications fairly consistently, Monday through Friday. As time passed, however, the purpose of the meditations grew to become more of a soul searching nature versus simple, feel good messages.

Whenever I sat at the computer preparing for a MEDITATION, I asked God what He would have me share. I relied on His leadership regarding what to send. Sometimes it was one word, other times one sentence. At times, there were poems, scriptures, notes from sermons, and even health tips. Testimonies, however, were what I enjoyed sharing most. I'm a firm believer in "If He did it for me, He will do it for you." I was eager to tell of God's goodness so others could be inspired. Although the end results of the testimonies were praiseworthy, I intentionally revealed my most intimate feelings and struggles experienced during these tests.

As the years passed, and the distribution list grew, I frequently received replies regarding the impact of specific messages. Even after I discontinued the emails, I knew someday I would compile them into a usable format so other individuals could be blessed as well. Several years elapsed before I was able to make any significant progress in this area. Recently, I was moved by a strong belief that *now* was the time to accomplish this task. Total reliance upon God was essential to bring this project to fruition. I knew very little about the publishing industry. I didn't know how to organize the book, what it should be entitled, or which messages to include. I determined to put aside my self-effort, which had gotten me very little progress in the past, and fully rely on God's ability to work through me.

This entire project has been—and still is—a walk of faith, trusting God every step of the way. Similar to many of the messages I shared through the meditations, this finished product exists only because of the Grace of God. I am not an author by profession; I don't have a large platform, and I have no professional credentials or letters following my name. The only credit I profess to have is I am a born-again believer who is convinced that when you place *all* your trust in God, the impossible becomes possible.

While reviewing the numerous pages of material I had compiled, I concluded it would be best if I created two separate books: one solely for testimonies and another for the many nuggets God spoke during the eight years of distributing the meditations. Although another book will be comprised of the nuggets, each testimony herein includes one nugget as an additional point of contemplation.

There's Nothing Like a Testimony is volume one of my attempt to organize the meditations and put them in a format that can be shared with others. No matter where you are in your spiritual life, I believe the truths in these testimonies will prove to be relevant resources. For some, they will reinforce current beliefs. Others will renew intimate times with God. Still, others may receive revelations that have never been disclosed before. Even as I was composing this book, I found myself reflecting on many of the messages and reminding myself that I am just the messenger.

As you read through these pages, I trust specific words, questions, and even entire testimonies will cause you to ponder the truths they reveal. There are numerous opportunities for reflection. Consider them. Know that God is not a respecter of persons. If He did it for me, He will do it for you!

Hearing His Will

Dear friend, listen well to my words;
tune your ears to my voice.
—Proverbs 4:20 the message

For the past few months, I've attempted to tune back into God and stop being so easily distracted away from Him. Not long ago, I was on a mission to learn how to hear God's voice. After executing the principles I learned from a tape series on hearing and obeying God's voice, I began to recognize His voice more and more. Then I allowed my life to get too busy, and I let the practice of these principles slip. I wasn't "hearing from God" as often as I had been.

Recently, I resumed my mission to grow closer to God and hear His voice. While in church this past Sunday, I believe God told me to give $50 to a lady in the service. When I first had this thought, I had peace and believed it was God; however, I allowed my mind to start questioning. After church, I was engrossed in other things and left without sowing that seed. As soon as I got home, I called my husband, who was still at church, and told him what I believed God had said. I asked him to give the lady the money. He willingly agreed and sowed the seed.

Yesterday—three days later—my husband and I received an envelope in the mail. Inside was a monetary gift for us in the amount of $57. God not only gave us back what we had sown, but He also gave us more! This experience was so exciting to me because I recalled how I was hearing from God before, so I was overjoyed about being in tune to my Father again.

I pray this testimony blesses you. We must be able to hear from God. We are His hands and feet in this earthly realm. He wants to use us to accomplish His will here. Being able to hear His voice is the key to carrying out that will.

※

*God is always talking,
but are we always listening?*

What's Your Motive?

> For we speak as messengers approved by God to be entrusted
> with the Good News. Our purpose is to please God, not
> people. He alone examines the motives of our hearts.
> —1 Thessalonians 2:4 NLT

It has become customary to include a label or card when giving a gift. Likewise, when we make contributions to certain fundraising efforts, a record is usually kept of our giving. Many of us probably even grew up with the mentality that the recipient of a gift *needed to know* it came from us. Labeling a gift and receiving a record of your giving are common practices. Despite this fact, according to biblical principles, it does not actually matter whether the person or organization to which we give is aware of our gift or not. The only one who truly needs this knowledge is God.

Matthew 6:1–4 explains how we should not create a spectacle when we give to a needy person. Instead, God who sees what we do in private will reward us in the open. Please don't take this principle to the extreme. I'm not trying to put anyone into bondage. The essential point concerns intent. What is your motive when you give? Motive is God's concern. Many times, it's inevitable that the recipient has knowledge of what we gave in a specific situation. Again, the fundamental question is what was your heart's condition at the time of your giving?

We must perform a self-analysis and rid ourselves of the "I gave" mentality. After all, we are only managers of God's assets here on Earth. If you find you are giving only to receive—not because the love of God motivates you—ask God for help in this area. See 1 Corinthians 1:1–3. LOVE must be the motivating factor behind why we do what we do. The next time you prepare to sow a seed, remember to ask yourself, "Am I about to sow this seed out of love, or is some other selfish reason motivating me?" Be sure your motive is pure so that God can return your seed back to you "pressed down, shaken together, and running over" (Luke 6:38 AMP).

Remember the only one who has to know what we give, how much we give, and to whom we give is God. As a matter of fact, He should be the One telling us *what* to give, *how much* to give, and *to whom* to give in the first place.

Are you acting out of a pure heart?

Is That You, God?

My sheep recognize my voice, and I know
them, and they follow me.
—John 10:27 TLB

On the way to have my car serviced, I was listening to a gospel CD. As I turned into the dealership, I had the thought to insert one of my pastor's tapes so that whoever set foot in the car would hear it upon entering. I was surprised by the thought but quickly acted on it and made the switch.

After the service on the car was completed, I approached my vehicle just as a young man had finished parking it. His first words to me were, "Who is the minister on that tape?" I immediately knew it was the Holy Spirit who had prompted me to insert the tape. I could hardly contain myself. This young man told me he thought he knew of the minister. He began to describe our church and asked where it was located. I inquired whether he had ever visited. He said he hadn't but expressed a desire to come. He mentioned that his mom watched my pastor on television all the time. We exchanged a few more words and ended our conversation.

As I pulled out of the dealership, all I could do was smile and tell God how awesome He is! For those who know me, I'm sure you can envision excited me traveling down the road grinning from ear to ear. Shortly thereafter, I began to think... *What if I hadn't yielded to the leading of the Holy Spirit?* For all I know, that young man or someone in his family is destined to become a member of our church or may need to hear the specific Word that will come forth when they visit. I began to reflect on how important it is for us to be able to hear from God. He has a master plan, and we are the agents He uses to carry it out.

I believe all God wants is for us to ask Him to direct our paths and for us to yield to His guidance through the promptings of the Holy Spirit. He will lead us every step of the way. I believe we will begin to see increase in every area of our lives, especially in our hearing from Him. How will we know if that voice we hear is God or not unless we step out and do whatever we believe He is speaking? Without a doubt, the best time to test your hearing is when your action will not affect anybody else. Just think…it didn't hurt anyone for me to follow through on that thought and pop in the tape. Because I acted, now I know that "thought" was, in fact, God speaking to me. Acting out on what we believe we've heard is the only way we're going to know His voice.

He wants to use you. Will you let Him?

Would Love Do That?

Whatever you do, do it with kindness and love.
—1 Corinthians 16:14 TLB

Last weekend, we had a Women's Breakfast at my church. A friend of mine had planned to attend. She would be arriving after me, so I offered to save her a seat. I was able to reserve two seats; however, one of the chairs would need to be turned around to see the stage. Admittedly, I put my belongings in the seat from which I would be able to see without difficulty.

Before the breakfast began, we had corporate prayer. While praying, God revealed to me what I had done. I had not acted in love because love prefers the other person. Having another individual inconvenienced is not something God would do, and it certainly is not an act of love. Needless to say, when prayer ended, I told my friend to sit in my chair, and I moved to the other seat. I was so thankful to God for revealing this to me. I couldn't do anything but smile.

Selfish acts, such as rushing ahead of another person, choosing something that looks better for yourself and giving a less attractive item to someone else, not sharing, and not considering others' feelings are all seeds of selfishness. When we don't prefer the other person or make sure his or her needs are met above our own, we can expect the same actions to be displayed toward us.

Love is such a thought-provoking subject. I believe we would be amazed at how selfish we are if we examined our actions more closely.

I challenge you to walk in love today:
- If you and another driver approach a parking space at the same time, sow a seed; let the other person have the space.
- If there is one doughnut left in the break room, sow a seed; let someone else have it.
- If you have only one piece of gum left and someone asks you for it, sow a seed; give it to him.
- If someone needs you to cover her desk for a little while, sow a seed; fill in for her.
- If you and your co-worker order the same sandwich for lunch and get back to the office only to discover one of the sandwiches has something on it that neither of you ordered, sow a seed; let the co-worker have the right one.

Sow seeds of love today, and you will reap an abundant harvest!

Your alphabet lesson for today: J, K, L

Joy
Kindness
Love

Baskets for Blessing

You will be a blessing [dispensing good to others].
—GENESIS 12:2 AMP

Earlier this month, I heard a minister on television issue a challenge to give away or "sow" something every day for thirty days. During my prayer time this morning, the Lord reminded me to give some baskets I own to someone else. He had instructed me to do it yesterday, but I was honestly hoping I had misunderstood.

The reason I'm sharing this with you is because of the following statement: We cannot allow ourselves to own anything that we are not willing to give up or sow at God's command. These baskets were not very expensive, but they were unique. I've never seen any like them before. The sad part is that I bought them before I was married, and I've been married almost four years! I had never even taken the tags off. I was holding on to them because I thought I might use them one day. Obviously, one day has not come.

God showed me with this little situation how important it is to realize that *every*thing we own belongs to Him. We have to be willing to sow *any*thing at His command. I couldn't believe the feelings and thoughts I had after I realized God definitely wanted me to give away the baskets. Yes, I'm only talking about *baskets*!

All I can do is thank God for the lesson in this small matter. I also realize that on the other side of my obedience is my increase. God has spiritual laws in place that will bring whatever we sow back to us. I view giving like an investment; it's a seed I plant for my future. Don't ever view giving as a loss; always see it as a gain.

I'm sure we all have possessions we're holding on to, thinking we might use them later. However, more often than not, years pass and later has still not come. We must take our minds off ourselves and get focused on blessing others. We are blessed to be a blessing!

Remember: We own nothing. God owns everything.

Have you surrendered all?

Share His Love

Little children, let us stop just saying we love people;
let us really love them, and show it by our actions.
—1 John 3:18 TLB

We must be ever mindful that God has a higher plan for us than we have for ourselves. Yesterday, I had several tasks to accomplish in the morning. After I finished a few of them, the idea came to me to visit an automotive shop. I needed to obtain an estimate for some required services on my car. Obtaining a quote was not in my plan for the morning at all. Nevertheless, since I believed God to have those major repairs done debt free, I decided to go. All the way there, I was thanking God for favor and for whatever He wanted to do for me to get what I needed done.

Once I entered the shop, I was greeted by an extremely personable gentleman. I was saying to myself, "I know I'm going to get favor in this place." When I arrived, he was working on a van that belonged to a lady who was visiting the city. She had come in town to attend her brother-in-law's funeral. The mechanics didn't know when her car would be fixed, and the funeral service was that day. She had some running around to do and had no other means of transportation. Because she had misplaced her driver's license, the rental company was not willing to rent her a car. As you can see, she had quite a few challenges facing her.

When I heard of her woes, I began to think that maybe this lady was why my schedule was rearranged—maybe she was the reason I was sitting in this shop. I asked God if I was supposed to do anything in this situation. I began a conversation with her. To make a long story short, we talked about many different things including her predicament, her family, and the importance of being a part of a church. As I was talking to her, tears filled her eyes. I asked if she was okay. Her response was, "I just can't believe you're talking to me." I was taken aback by her reply, but I knew then that she was the reason God had me go to that shop. I was there to show this lady the love of God.

As I was driving away, I expressed to God how good He is. I was in such awe of how He does things. I prayed for the lady and her family. I couldn't help but think about how we should always be sensitive to our spirits and follow these little nudges we receive. I also couldn't believe how I was selfishly thinking on the way to the shop that the trip was about me. On the other hand, I was quite pleased that I put my own agenda aside and allowed God to use me. After doing some comparative shopping, it appears I did receive my favor, too. Praise God! He is good!

Take the time to really listen.
You'd be surprised how much your
devoted ears would mean.

Rules of the World

> For God has not given us a spirit of fear, but of
> power and of love and of a sound mind.
> —2 Timothy 1:7 NKJV

Yesterday, while on the way to pick up my husband, I noticed a lady walking down the road. She was dressed in a suit and carrying a portfolio in her hands as if she had been to an interview. I was driving through a business district, so I didn't think it strange to see this lady. However, after picking up my husband, I noticed the woman was still walking. I asked Rod if we could pick her up. We turned around and asked if she'd like a ride. She hesitated a moment and then said, "Yes."

While traveling to her house, she explained her car had broken down. She had not been able to reach anyone to come pick her up. She continued to express her gratitude and appreciation for the ride. We said we were just trying to be a blessing and that God is good. She then mentioned she had been praying the whole time. Once we arrived at her apartment, I realized she would have been walking a rather long way.

I shared this story with you because many times we allow the "rules of the world" to hinder our acts of kindness. Many people would probably tell me I was crazy to give a ride to someone who was walking. To that I would say, "I let God be my guide." It was obvious to us that God used us yesterday to do His work and answer that lady's prayer.

Always be sensitive to the leading of the Holy Spirit. Don't allow fear to keep you from doing what you know

God told you to do. Remember, our angels and the Holy Spirit are always with us. Our inner peace will tell us whether we should or should not act in a particular situation. Don't allow the rules of the world to cause you to miss out on being a blessing in the name of Jesus.

Would you want something that didn't come from God?
Something that He didn't give you?
Well, why did you take it?
(See today's scripture.)

Seed for the Sower

> And [God] Who provides seed for the sower and bread for eating will also provide and multiply your [resources for] sowing and increase the fruits of your righteousness [which manifests itself in active goodness, kindness, and charity].
> —2 Corinthians 9:10 AMP

A few months ago, my husband and I decided to revisit the principles we had learned in a personal finance class we'd taken. We created a vision that listed specific monthly amounts we wanted to sow into four different areas. When we produced the vision, I was a volunteer for the ministry where we took the class. Subsequently, the head of the ministry asked if God had spoken to me about working there. Without getting into all the details, I am currently a part-time employee at that ministry.

To be honest, when I first accepted the position and realized what I would be making, my natural mind began to think of all the things I could do with the extra money. God quickly reminded me and my husband (who was having a few thoughts of his own) of the vision we had written down. Regretfully, I cannot tell you I was jumping for joy when I recalled our vision. However, after I thought about God's promise of a harvest from seeds, I realized sowing this money would not be a loss. We would be planting precious seed from which we could certainly expect an abundant harvest.

Once I receive my checks for the month, pay my tithes, and sow the amounts in those four areas, I'll have $2.36 remaining. I shared this figure because I want you to realize that God gives seed to the sower. God knew my husband and I were sowers, so He knew He could trust us to do what He desired with the money. Obviously, fulfilling that vision was exactly what He wanted us to do.

When we take care of God's kingdom, He will always take care of us. One of the things I had thought about being able to do with the extra money was shopping. Rod and I hadn't purchased anything new in a while because we were focused on getting out of debt, but my God always has something up His sleeve...

Last weekend, my parents and an aunt came into town. All I'll say is that when they left, I had four new outfits, a pair of shoes, money for alterations, and some hair care products I wanted. To add to that, my husband, who had been out of town, returned home with two purses for me. He also allowed me to exchange something else he had bought for some shoes that I needed. GOD IS GOOD TO ME!

When God brings increase into your hands, don't suddenly get amnesia concerning its purpose. Do not neglect to fulfill the vision. My husband and I were determined to carry out the vision even though it left only $2.36; however, that $2.36 vanishes in comparison to the gifts God gave me last weekend. I also had to remind myself that that job is not my source. God is my Source, and He has His own way of getting to me what I need and desire. Just be obedient, and God will take care of the rest.

Can God trust you?

It Can Happen Just Like That!

> And the man jumped up, grabbed his mat, and walked out through the stunned onlookers. They were all amazed and praised God, exclaiming, "We've never seen anything like this before!"
> —Mark 2:12 NLT

Yesterday, someone I know shared with me she had sold her home. We had just been discussing her house the day before. She didn't mention anything about selling the home or that it was even on the market.

She told me she and her husband had been toying with the idea of selling, but she had decided she would like to remain in her home. Her husband later suggested they put the house on the market at a much higher price just to see what would happen. Well, before the "For Sale" sign was posted in the yard, their agent had someone who desired to see the home. Much to their surprise, the man who toured the house wanted to purchase it, and he wanted it immediately!

Quite naturally, the homeowner was concerned about what to do with her furniture. Please understand I'm referring to an over half a million dollar house. She didn't want to put everything in storage, and she had no desire to go through the hassle of selling anything. Given the time she had to move out, she was perplexed over what to do. She received another call and the man who was purchasing the home also wanted to buy some of the furniture. He asked if he could have a second tour to identify pieces he'd like to acquire. By the time he finished, he had decided to buy the home and everything in it! All of these decisions occurred within a couple of days.

I was in total awe when she shared this testimony with me. During my prayer time this morning, I was meditating on what happened to her, and God spoke this to me: "When God is in it, it can happen just like that—with the snap of your fingers!"

Think about this: One day you're living in and enjoying your home and just playing with the idea of selling it. Then, the next day, you've sold it at a much higher price than you thought possible, sold everything in it, and have two weeks to find somewhere to live. Now, all I know is…When God is in it, it can happen just like that!

Don't limit Him based on what you see.

I am a Creator

So God created man in His own image, in the image and likeness
of God He created him; male and female He created them.
—Genesis 1:27 amp

What I'm about to share will probably sound elementary to you, but it was revelation knowledge to me. During my prayer time, I was thanking and acknowledging God for being The Creator. Then, the thought came to me that I am made in His image; therefore, I am a creator. I am creative! God created the sun, the moon, the trees, the wind, the rain, all the good things we see and don't see. This Creator—the One in whose image I am made—fashioned these things, and I have the same ability!

Realizing I have God's creative abilities was revelation knowledge to me because I've always said that I am not a very creative person. I know now that making that confession all my life was counterproductive to discovering my God-given imaginative abilities. Conversely, when I started thinking about The Creator this morning and how I am made in His image, I had a brand-new view of my potential to be creative. I simply need to acknowledge and place a demand on those abilities.

Thus, in whatever area you need help, look to the Father. We are made in His image. No matter what it is, if God has it or can do it, you have it and you can do it!

*His abilities are your abilities, so why
did you say you couldn't do it?*

My Real Employer

> Whatever may be your task, work at it heartily (from the soul), as [something done] for the Lord and not for men.
> —COLOSSIANS 3:23 AMP

We must remember we can do absolutely nothing without God. Anything we accomplish or attain is solely as a result of His empowerment. In Him, we live and move and have our being (Acts 17:28). I am about to be very transparent with you, and I believe my frankness will bless you.

I work part time as the accountant for an outreach ministry. Over the last few months, I've been involved in automating the accounting system. I was working on a particular area and realized we needed to make a specific adjustment. To reach this conclusion, I analyzed quite a bit of information to obtain the final number. I had run a lengthy adding machine tape and was using it in certain comparisons. On the tape, I had made notes and marks that were legible but definitely not as neat as they could have been. After noticing the messy appearance of the tape, I began to think of how *my employer* might react to it; therefore, I reran the numbers and made an Excel spreadsheet that detailed the components of the data. I put a packet together with the spreadsheet on top and all the supporting documentation below it. If I may say so myself, the finished product was rather impressive.

Here is the good part. I had a conference scheduled with my employer to review the progress in the accounting department. At the meeting, I began to discuss the status of the automation project and point out particular items I had discovered. I suggested that from my calculations, a specific adjustment needed to be made. I showed her the top page with the bottom line figure. She understood what I explained and didn't ask any more questions. I must admit I was indeed tempted to show her all the work I had done to arrive at this bottom line figure, especially the coded register tape that I had so diligently done over. The way the conversation was going I could have led into showing her all my backup work, but the Holy Spirit restrained me and quickly helped me realize that I was working for *Him* and not for *my employer*—that I needed to be concerned about being pleasing in His eyes, that He had seen what I had done, and that this was all that mattered.

I learned a priceless lesson that day. Many of us say we're working for or carrying out deeds for God. I wonder, though, whether our attitude is always one of not being concerned about recognition from any person, organization, or source other than God. Bear in mind, God sees all things. He is our rewarder. We need to have an excellent spirit at all times because He is watching. As I stated at the beginning, we can do absolutely nothing without Him.

Who do you work for?

The Thankfulness List

Be thankful in all circumstances, for this is God's
will for you who belong to Christ Jesus.
—1 Thessalonians 5:18 NLT

Take a moment to write down 10 things for which you are thankful. It may not be the Thanksgiving holiday, but we still need to express our gratitude toward God. Please try to think outside of the customary items of food, clothing, and shelter. Just this morning, I found myself thanking God for some things I don't often consider. The following are three examples of unusual things for which I give thanks.

One day I was driving down the road, and I saw someone running across the street, dashing through cars and trying to wave down a bus so he wouldn't miss it. I thought to myself how grateful I am to God for allowing me to have a car to drive—to be able to go where I want, when I want. My heart sincerely went out to that person. I pondered how he may have felt had he missed his bus.

While in the grocery store the other day, I saw someone from my church whom I knew didn't have a car. She was rearranging her groceries to be able to carry them easily on the bus. I asked if she'd like a ride, and she was noticeably thankful. After I dropped her off, I again started to think of how God has allowed me to have so many conveniences. I then thought of how I probably should have given her the opportunity to go back in the store for more items because she most likely only purchased what she could carry.

I was also thinking about how some people live their

entire lives in an apartment. Don't misunderstand me. I have no problem whatsoever with apartment living. An apartment equals no mortgage. (Yay!) I was just considering how I had always been blessed to live in a house with a front and back yard. It had never dawned on me that there are some people who have only experienced apartment living and have never lived in a house. Again, I just thought of how thankful I should be and how thankful I am.

Sometimes we forget to express gratitude for things such as these. Many of us have always had a multitude of conveniences all our lives. It's sometimes a shock to realize what others have never had. Therefore, once more I ask you to take a moment to create a thankfulness list. Take the time, right now, to thank your heavenly Father.

In the everyday rush of life,
pause to give God glory and thanks.
He delights in our praise.

A Willing Heart

> I [the Lord] will instruct you and teach you in the way you
> should go; I will counsel you with My eye upon you.
> —Psalm 32:8 AMP

I take two girls to church with me on Sundays. They attend our children's ministry. Last week's lesson was on God's system of operation—seedtime and harvest. An incident occurred yesterday that enabled me to reinforce what they had learned.

Someone I know called to tell me she wanted to sow a seed into my life. I had no idea what seed she was referring to, but we decided I would pick it up after service on Sunday. The seed was *The Leadership Bible*. I desired one but hadn't purchased it yet. Naturally, I was ecstatic. Once I calmed down, I went back to my car where the girls were waiting. I realized now was the perfect opportunity to show them how God's system works and how quickly they can reap a harvest off their seeds.

The day before was the youngest girl's birthday. She had turned 10, and I gave her a children's Bible as a present. I explained to them how I had just sown a seed—a Bible—as a birthday gift and how I had just received a harvest of a Bible. Surely, this chain of events was a divine set up. I was so excited! They were greatly impacted. I believe they were able to see that whatever you desire to harvest or receive, you must sow or give.

I was elated over what had just happened. I had my leadership Bible, and God had just used me to help teach the girls a vital life lesson. Prior to this example, I had been trying to think of things I could do with them to help influence their lives. (I hadn't been around many children.) God showed me that everyday occurrences could be used to have a lasting impact. Isn't God good! He wants us to know that as long as we have a willing heart and step out to do what we believe is His will, He'll be there to help us along the way.

*I'm the best there is at
on-the-job training.*
—God

No Job... NO PROBLEM

He does not fear bad news, nor live in dread of what may happen.
For he is settled in his mind that Jehovah will take care of him.
—PSALM 112:7 TLB

On January 16, 2001, I sent out a MEDITATION that read: *No matter what happens today... SMILE! Remember, no matter what happens, immediately respond with a SMILE.* As I turned into my complex after work that day, God reminded me of this MEDITATION. It rose up intensely inside me, and I began to SMILE.

Once inside my apartment, I walked to my computer and noticed my husband Rod had been working on his résumé. I remembered he had tried to call me at work earlier in the day. He had not been looking for another job, so I assumed something must have changed regarding his employment status. I called to confirm my suspicion. He explained things were slow at his job, so the company had to let him and another contractor go.

After I got off the phone, God immediately reminded me of that MEDITATION. I couldn't do anything but SMILE and be in awe of the love of my Father. I wholeheartedly believe He gave me that word especially for us. I had so much peace. I can't even explain it. I was totally at peace. I just knew God was going to take care of everything. Shortly after we married, Rod allowed me to quit my job, so I haven't worked full time since 1996. As a result, we basically "live" off his salary. Regardless, I was certain God was going to provide.

Naturally, my husband began to submit his résumé and

take the manly steps as head of the household. Jehovah Jireh, as always, showed up. After being out of work about a week and a half, Rod received a phone call from a vice-president (whom he had never met or contacted) at his previous employer. The VP expressed he had been hearing positive remarks about my husband and someone suggested he reach out to see if he would be interested in returning. Rod ultimately accepted the offer and began work that Monday, two weeks after he had been released from the contract position.

Believe it or not, the position my husband accepted was the same one he vacated when he left the company two months prior. Other than a few more human resource responsibilities and having to report to someone new, he was back in his old position. I believe God honored the integrity of Rod's heart and held that position vacant just so he could return to this company. I am a firm believer that when we desire to please God, He will make sure we stay in His will. The best part about this story is that my husband had been in technical recruiter positions his entire career but had a desire to acquire more human resource training. This "new" position offered HR training, a higher salary, and a signing bonus. Look at God!

When Rod left his old position, the company was in the process of restructuring. No one at his company could tell him with any certainty what the future held. Unquestionably, he liked his job and the people but felt it best he leave. As a side note, during the two months my husband held the contract position, God enabled us to significantly pay down our debt. Not many days from now, we will be totally debt free.

I intentionally did not tell anyone, especially my family,

when my husband was released from his contract position because I wanted to see God move. I wanted to rely on Him entirely to provide. If our situation had reached a point where we needed something, I didn't want my family to be my source. I wanted God to prove He truly is our Provider. And that is exactly what He did.

Look at it this way...It's just an opportunity for you to manifest the Word of God—an opportunity for you to demonstrate His power in the earth—an opportunity to prove His Word and give Him the glory. See the positive in all things.

I'm Healed and That's That

> So let us seize and hold fast and retain without wavering the hope we cherish and confess and our acknowledgement of it, for He Who promised is reliable (sure) and faithful to His word.
> —Hebrews 10:23 AMP

For the past few days, I've had some allergy/cold-like symptoms. They started with my throat hurting every time I swallowed. Then, my nasal passages became slightly congested, and yesterday, I began having pains in my left ear. It felt as if my ear was clogged up, and every so often, I'd have sharp pains that caused me to cringe. As the day progressed, the pain grew worse and more constant. I was absolutely miserable. All I wanted to do was cry, as if that would have helped.

I visited the pharmacist for a consultation. Because I had such pain in my ear, she said the discomfort was probably due to an ear infection. She recommended I see my doctor and suggested Actifed to dry up the drainage. I had to serve at a finance class that night, so Actifed was not an option. Without purchasing any medicine, I drove back to work. The pain grew worse. I was trying anything I could think of for relief. I was confessing my healing scriptures, but honestly, the pain became even more piercing. My ear felt as if it needed to pop. Add pain to that, and the situation was almost unbearable. I was pleading to God for help.

I had a thought to ask two other people in the office to agree with me in prayer. They were staunch believers in the power of prayer. I was certain they would have no problem acting out on the Word and coming into agreement with me. Because I had not requested prayer in this way before, I admit I was a bit hesitant. Nonetheless, I made my request and they accepted. We held hands in the office and began to pray in the Spirit. After we had prayed for a few seconds, one of the people began to pray in English, confessing the Word of God on healing and our rights as the righteousness of God. I could feel my ear begin to clear up. She acted out on the Word and cupped her hands over my ears. Within seconds, my ear completely cleared up, and the pain ceased. When we finished praying, tears of joy were flowing as I thanked God and my co-workers for agreeing with me.

I must share the rest of the story. Shortly after the manifestation of my healing, the clogging and pain returned. I immediately rebuked Satan and was determined not to give in to his second attack against my body. All I could think was that it was up to me to keep my healing. I had made up my mind that no matter what I felt in my ear, from that point forward, I was healed. I knew it. I continued to reflect on my prayer experience. Undoubtedly, God had healed me. The symptoms continued, but I was unwavering in my stance on healing. I continued serving, confessing my scriptures, and doing what I needed to do, no matter what my body felt. The pain eventually left. I can't even tell you when. And as I write this testimony to you, I have absolutely no pain or stuffiness in my ear. God is Jehovah Rophe, my Healer!

You have to BELIEVE God. You can't expect anything to happen unless you really BELIEVE.

Right Place, Right Time

> The Lord directs the steps of the godly. He
> delights in every detail of their lives.
> —Psalm 37:23 NLT

Last week, I celebrated my 29th birthday. PRAISE THE LORD!!! I had to work all day, and we had a staff meeting that night. My husband had practice for his boys' baseball team, too. Instead of trying to work around our schedules and rush to have a quick dinner, I decided we could celebrate the next day.

At each of our staff meetings, we collect an offering to sow toward someone's debt cancellation. A first and second name is drawn each meeting. There are three requirements to be eligible: (1) The person must be present; (2) The person must be a consistent giver; and (3) The person must have his Rapid Debt Reduction Worksheet.

We finished receiving the offering, and the first person's name was announced. Sadly, she had grabbed the wrong purse and didn't have her Rapid Debt Reduction Worksheet with her. And who was the second name? You guessed it. I was the alternate for that night. All everyone heard was a blaring scream. That was the best birthday gift I could have received. We only have one bill remaining, and it is almost paid off. The offering that night put a $510 dent in Mr. MasterCard's balance. I PRAISE GOD! He knows how much we desire to be totally debt free, and I believe He allowed my name to be called just to show us He is going to pay off the remaining balance in supernatural time.

THANK GOD I was at the right place at the right time.

Imagine if I hadn't shown up just because it was my birthday. You know we do that sometime. God is so good!

My husband and I had also made an appointment for a chef to prepare meals for us this week. On Friday, someone I work with advised me God had told her to sow that seed into my life as a birthday gift. She immediately went to her checkbook, wrote the check out to the chef, and gave it to me. Let me tell you why this gift is significant. This person had suggested Rod and I step out and begin using the chef once a month (versus each week) to get a vision of having a personal chef. I didn't act immediately because we were still working on this last debt, and I was being extremely frugal. In the end, we decided to go ahead and treat ourselves. And look at God; He stepped in and took care of the chef's fee just like that!

Okay, I just have to tell this one last thing. My parents mentioned they had mailed my birthday card. However, I didn't get it on my birthday. When I checked the mailbox the next day, there were four cards inside. Can you believe each card had a check in it? Money cometh to us NOW in Jesus' name. Okay, I'll close now. You know how I get when I talk about my Jesus.

Depend on Him to help you make right choices.

A Trip to the Airport

> For those who honor Me I will honor, and those
> who despise Me shall be lightly esteemed.
> —1 Samuel 2:30 amp

I had agreed to take a couple I know to the airport yesterday. I attended the early morning service at church, and on the way back home, God started dealing with me about the appearance of my car. Rain was in the forecast, so I tried and tried to talk myself out of the need to wash my car. It didn't work. I realized the right thing would be to wash it, regardless of the forecast.

I had the car washed, but when I got back home, I noticed the tires were still dirty. My husband had to stay at church after the first service, so I grabbed the bucket and cleaned them myself. Then, I looked inside the car and realized I needed to do a bit of work on the interior in order to have an excellent finished product. As I was cleaning my windows, God pointed out that if I had to pick up the minister where I am employed, there is no way I would pick her up in a dirty car, so why should I do less for anyone else? I also thought I should be even more concerned if I had to pick up my husband. Sometimes we treat the people closest to us with the least importance. I'm aware God is a God of excellence, and I believe He was pleased with what I was doing. For this reason, I said to myself, "God is going to honor my excellence." Little did I know what I was really saying.

The car was finally clean, and I was about to throw on my normal jeans, T-shirt, and sneakers. Once again, God began to deal with me. This time the topic was my attire. He reminded me that this couple I was taking to the airport seldom ever dressed so plainly. Moreover, if it had been my employer, I never would have picked her up dressed that casual. Therefore, I upgraded my usual attire as well.

When I arrived at their home, just as I had expected, this couple looked polished and prosperous. I was about 15 minutes early, but they were packed and ready to go. By this time, the sun was shining brightly, and there wasn't a cloud in the sky. I whipped my clean Camry around in the driveway and popped the trunk. I stepped out and began sharing in the excitement about their trip.

The couple began to explain a few things they had asked me to check on while they were gone. Right before we got in the car, the wife told me that they wanted to give my husband and me something. I told her that was absolutely unnecessary, but she insisted and said, "The check is already made out." While I continued to talk, I heard her mention that she had written the check out to someone else. Then I looked down and saw who she was referring to. They had written a check payable to the chef we use, so we could be blessed with another evening of meals prepared by him. PRAISE GOD! I was so in shock. This couple lives practically right around the corner, and the airport is not even 15 minutes away. Did God honor my excellent spirit or what? I was just in awe of what He had done. I was so glad that I lined up and did what I knew was right, even though my flesh did not necessarily feel like it.

After I dropped the couple at the airport, I was reflecting on what had happened and thanking God. I began to meditate on how important it is to have a spirit of excellence and not to be a respecter of persons. This couple was going away for an extended vacation. I could have set a negative tone for the start of their trip by picking them up in a dirty car and looking as if I had just gotten out of bed.

It is so awesome how God *truly* honored me because cooking is on the list of my least favorite things to do. He is AWESOME!

Be faithful in the little.

The Desires of My Heart

The desire of the righteous will be granted.
—PROVERBS 10:24 NKJV

Wednesday morning, I had a thought to go to a mall I've been saying I would visit for the longest time. It's only about 15 minutes away, but I'd never been there. I just had this unexplainable desire to go that particular day. I went to morning Bible study and had decided that if I felt like it after service, I would go. I made a stop right after church and was almost about to go home, but I still felt this yearning to visit that mall. While I was in the car thinking about what I was going to do, I said, "Lord, there must be something at that mall for me." Needless to say, I went to the mall.

When I walked inside, it appeared almost deserted. The prospect of finding whatever it was God had for me looked somewhat slim. I strolled along noticing the names of the stores. Nothing caught my attention until I saw a shoe store. During the prior weeks, I had been looking for a particular brand of sandal. I had already been in this specific chain store, but I decided to take a second look. They had an abundance of sandals; however, I still didn't see what I was looking for. I tried on several pairs and had a couple boxes in my hands.

I started to walk through the rest of the store and noticed more sandals in the back. These were all between 30% and 50% off. Bargain shopper that I am, I looked over these rather closely. To my surprise, I saw the brand name I had been seeking. The sandal on display was quite appealing; however, only four boxes were left on the shelf. My shoe size is very common, so it's usually the first to go. But not this day. Remember, God had me in that mall for a reason. I looked at the boxes and found my size. I immediately started grinning and whispered, "This is why I came to this mall."

When I tried on the sandals, they felt wonderful; however, I noticed the strap on the left sandal was sticking out and not fitting snuggly like the right side. I was sure these shoes were the reason why God had me in this mall, so I was puzzled by this discovery. These were the sandals I had been searching for. They were already reasonably priced, and there was an additional 30% off. I couldn't understand why that strap wasn't in its proper place. While standing, I tried to move it, but it wouldn't budge. I kept looking at them in the mirror and walking around confident that these were my shoes, but I didn't want to buy them with an unaligned left strap. I sat down on a bench and attempted to adjust the strap again. This time, it moved right into place. I grinned immensely and started giving all kinds of praises and thank you's to the Holy Spirit. As you probably guessed, I bought the sandals, but that's not the end of the story…

As I was leaving the mall, prancing along in awe of my Father, I saw another chain store that had two dresses I liked. I had refused to purchase them a week or two prior because they were regular price, but I had been thinking about them ever since. Don't you know my God had one of those dresses on sale for 40% off. He is so good!

To top that off, I ate lunch at a Mongolian grill that had the best lemon pepper chicken I had ever tasted. I had a SUPERB day.

I shared the details of my mall visit simply to say, please

be sensitive to the Holy Spirit. He knows all things. He knew the desire of my heart. He knew exactly where I could get it, and He knew the perfect time to show up to lay hold on it. Hallelujah!!

Lord, direct my steps today; lead me, guide me in Your perfect way.

A Reservation for Four, Please

> Rather, let our lives lovingly express truth [in all
> things, speaking truly, dealing truly, living truly].
> —EPHESIANS 4:15 AMP

Recently, Rod and I were on vacation with a number of family members. Four relatives, including my husband and me, had return flights earlier than the rest of our family. Because we were about two hours from the airport and our flights were 6:30 a.m. and 7:15 a.m., the four of us decided to lodge near the airport the night before we were to leave. I assumed the responsibility of making the reservation.

We started discussing our plans while on a van with the rest of our relatives. I had obtained rates from a couple of hotels I had called the night before. I explained how much the room would be for four people. Almost everyone in the van started ranting about my need to request the rate for only one or two people and leave it at that. Obviously, I was not in agreement. I announced that to make such a statement would be a lie, and I was not going to comply. I was strongly criticized for my viewpoint because "everybody" does not always give a true number of people in a room. I stood up for what I believed and allowed them to think that I was totally insane. Because of the city we were in, the hotel rates were already much higher than normal, so my obstinacy did not help matters. What happened? We ended up securing a hotel for the rate of one person. The hotel was running a special, which allowed up to four adults in a room for the price of one. LOOK AT GOD!

What makes this story so special is that one of the people

staying with us had seen me display my integrity about the number of individuals in a room in a past situation. She also saw how God honored my honesty in that setting. To summarize, when the reservation was made, one number of adults was given, but by the time sleeping arrangements were determined, the number had increased. After we checked into the room, I felt compelled to inform the lady at the front desk. Again, everyone insisted I was crazy. They even said I would have to pay the difference myself if there was a rate increase. I was not bothered by what they said. I knew I had to live by my own convictions. I proceeded downstairs to advise the desk clerk. You know my God showed out! I received favor, and there was no increase in our rate. PRAISE GOD!!

I shared these stories to encourage you to always stand up for what you believe. No matter how disturbing the remarks about you may become—even if you're standing by yourself—stand up for what you believe.

Don't compromise your beliefs.

Everything is Lovely

> God…gives life to the dead and calls those things
> which do not exist as though they did.
> —ROMANS 4:17 NKJV

I thought a good response to someone who asks how you're doing today would be, "Everything is lovely!"

My grandfather had melanoma cancer, which eventually took his life about a year ago. Recently, when we visited his daughter in California, I discovered that every time she called home to check on him, his reply would be, "Everything is lovely!"

My mom spent considerable time with my grandfather during his last days. I've heard her say that he never complained about his condition. Now, if a man who was in constant pain and basically bedridden can reply, "Everything is lovely"…

I must ask you, "How are you doing today?"

The kind of day you have is up to you.

Manifestation Time

> You shall also decide and decree a thing, and
> it shall be established for you; and the light
> [of God's favor] shall shine upon your ways.
> —Job 22:28 AMP

I went to lunch with a friend this past Saturday. We had a wonderful time of fellowship. We discussed our lives, the goodness of God, and how much God has in store for us. Her husband had dropped her off at the restaurant, so I took her home. Like many uplifting conversations, it seemed as if we couldn't bring ours to a close. Even after we arrived at her house, we sat in the car and continued to chat.

We were both seeking to be debt free, so that subject came up in our conversation. While casually talking about life, I mentioned that Rod and I had one small debt left. After I made that statement, my friend said, "If you don't mind me asking, how much is that debt?"

I told her I didn't mind and then replied, "About $1,000."

As we continued talking, the subject of this last debt came up again. This time, my friend became so excited that she immediately took out her checkbook! I asked her what she was doing. She said she and her husband needed to get in on the cancellation of our last debt. I was in total shock. Then, she started writing the check. I cautioned her concerning the need to speak with her husband first. She assured me he would be in total agreement. Amazingly, her phone rang, and it was her husband. I reiterated she needed to clear whatever she was about to do with him. She confidently told me he would probably tell her to write it for more. At this point, I had to get out of the car and walk around. I was so overcome by the awesomeness of my Father.

While my friend and her husband were talking, I was meandering in their backyard, thanking and praising God for whatever He was about to do. She got out of the car, came over to me, and said, "The Pauldins are totally debt free." Yes, you read it right; they wrote a check out to our credit card company for $1,000! Our confession of faith has now manifested. God is soooo good!!!

Over and over, the Bible instructs us to believe.
You don't have to earn His promises;
you just have to believe them.

He Showed Up With My Clothes

> And why worry about your clothing? Look at the lilies of the field and how they grow. They don't work or make their clothing, yet Solomon in all his glory was not dressed as beautifully as they are. And if God cares so wonderfully for wildflowers that are here today and thrown into the fire tomorrow, he will certainly care for you. Why do you have so little faith?
> —Matthew 6:28–30 NLT

I am currently four and a half months pregnant. At this time, there is very little in my wardrobe I can wear. I bought a few pieces a while back but still needed more. I was making remarks to my husband, implying he needed to give me the money to buy them. Every time I made a comment like that, God would remind me that my husband is not my source…He is.

It is often quite easy for us (especially housewives) to look to other people as our source. While pondering this issue, God reminded me of the scriptures in Matthew 6:25–31 where He tells us not to be concerned about clothing, so I had made a mental decision to meditate on God's Word and watch Him show up with my clothes. You know there's a testimony coming, right?

Before I had even come to this resolution, someone from church told me she wanted to bless me with a maternity dress. She called yesterday to find out if it would be okay to come by my apartment to "give me what God had blessed me with." Of course, I told her she was welcome. She arrived with a gift box and another bag in hand. She gave me the gift box which contained the dress. I tried it on; it fit perfectly!

Then, she said she had some more things for me. As I mentioned, I had seen the bag, but I assumed it contained clothes that someone was giving away. Much to my surprise, in addition to the dress, she had bought me two shirts, a turtleneck sweater, a pair of pants, and a casual suit. I was astonished. After all, I had just been thinking that I'm going to stop worrying about acquiring more clothes and depend on God to supply that need. Did He show out or what! And that's not all. Within the last couple days, I had a thought that I wanted to get something red. As my loving Father would have it, one of the shirts she bought me was red, and it was oh so cute! All I can say is God is good and He is Jehovah Jireh, my Provider.

As I was modeling the clothing, we talked about how one of the outfits would look great with a pair of boots. Once she arrived back home, she called to tell me she had three pairs of shoes to give me—one of which was a pair of boots she doesn't wear. Now, that is my Provider! He's AWESOME!!!

Depend on NOthing and NObody but God.

A Box of Blessings

And my God will liberally supply (fill to the full) your every
need according to His riches in glory in Christ Jesus.
—PHILIPPIANS 4:19 AMP

On November 8, I sent out a MEDITATION concerning my need for maternity clothing. I expressed how I had been looking to my husband to provide them but was reminded by God that He is my Source. I also shared the testimony about the clothing someone had purchased for me. Now, the blessing continues…

Ever since that time, as stated in Matthew 6:25–31, that care remained cast on God. I knew I needed more clothes, but I was not at all worried. I continued to wear what I had and didn't allow my limited number of maternity pieces to concern me.

A long-time family friend, who had a baby over a year ago, mentioned she had some maternity clothes to give me. I was a bit concerned, though, because she's extremely petite and a bit shorter than I am. I received the clothes on Saturday. I want you to know that I could wear EVERYTHING in the box. Some of the pants were even a tad too long on me, and all of the pieces were in excellent condition. There were about four two-piece outfits, two dress pant suits, six pairs of pants, and about four shirts. She even had some brand-new maternity pantyhose in there that I had hesitated to buy because they were so expensive. Do you realize that I don't have to buy anything else unless I just want to? GOD IS MY SOURCE!

And, you know my Father, of course, there's more. I

had been out of town, and when I returned, my husband surprised me with three brand-new pairs of shoes. All I could do was thank God and think of how good He is. To God be the glory!

※

God has you on His mind.

That's the One

The LORD is my strength and shield. I trust him with
all my heart. He helps me, and my heart is filled
with joy. I burst out in songs of thanksgiving.
—PSALM 28:7 NLT

You know I like to tell everything, so it's been concerning me that I never shared about the goodness of God regarding our move into the rental home where we now reside. Here goes…

First, finding the home in itself was an act of God. Rod and I had already notified our leasing office that we were not going to renew the apartment lease. Because this advice had to be submitted 60 days in advance, it was too early for us to have secured another residence.

We began our search by obtaining a listing from a local real estate office, looking through the newspaper, and observing signs along the road. We followed this process diligently from the time we submitted the termination notice. We had already set a budget, so we would flip through the information, mark the properties we were interested in, and drive by for a look. I am not exaggerating when I say that practically everything we saw was a big NO! We never stepped foot inside any of them. We were within 30 days of our move-out date and had not yet found a home. However, all along we had been sowing seed and naming it for God to lead us to the perfect home for us.

One Saturday, my husband and I drove separately to look at some homes we had identified in different parts of town. As we were driving off, I said a quick prayer and asked God to direct us. Time was winding down, but I knew our house was out there. Furthermore, I was certain God knew exactly where it was.

As Rod was traveling to see one of the houses on his list, he saw a small "For Rent" sign pointing down a side road. He turned down the road, and there it was—our new home. Rod immediately called the number on the sign to make an appointment for me to view the house.

We had planned to meet each other at the fitness center after we completed our lists. When my husband entered the gym, he told me he had found our house—that this one was it. Although he hadn't seen the inside, he just knew this was the one. The outside and location were exactly what we were looking for.

I later met with the wife of the couple who owned the house. She gave me a tour of the home. It had everything we wanted. While the owner and I were talking, I informed her that she would have no payment issues with us because we make a point to pay our bills on time. I also shared that we were out of debt. I believe our freedom from debt was refreshing news to her.

Rod and I met with the couple on a subsequent date. As you'd expect, they wanted to rent the home immediately; however, I told them we did not desire to make two lodging payments in the same month. We continued to converse and discovered they were Christians and attended church regularly as well. I honestly believe this meeting was all a divine set up because the homeowners had had challenges with some previous tenants, and this was the exact house we desired.

God's favor showed up because our landlords held the house for us almost a month. They also gave us the keys the same day we signed the lease—about 25 days before the start of the lease. The owners said we could go ahead and start moving our belongings in. Keep in mind, our rental period didn't officially begin until 25 days later! God is AWESOME!

Trust Him. He will lead you.

Don't Take That Shortcut

> Wise men and women are always learning,
> always listening for fresh insights.
> —Proverbs 18:15 the message

On Tuesday, I attended a Sales and Use Tax Seminar conducted by the Georgia Department of Revenue. It was scheduled to be held from 8:00 a.m. until 5:00 p.m. Someone I know recently started a business, so I asked if she would like to attend with me. Once I explained the class was on the north side of town (at least 45–50 minutes away), her decision was made. I suggested she could ride with me, but she was still not interested.

She stated that all I needed to do was visit the Regional Office. She commented that someone there could walk me through the form and explain everything I needed to know. I must admit that idea was quite tempting. After speaking with her and considering what she said, I had decided to forgo the seminar and visit the local office, but again, something—Someone—inside me didn't give me peace about that decision.

I decided to attend the seminar, and I have absolutely no regrets. I gained a wealth of knowledge. I'm confident I wouldn't have received this much information at the local office. I learned a valuable lesson: Trying to take shortcuts will usually cause you to miss out on something. After attending the class, I realized *I don't know what I don't know*; therefore, I would not even have known what I needed to ask a person at the local office. One important nugget I picked up at the seminar was that I did not have to pay sales tax for goods I purchase to be resold. I was absolutely oblivious to this law. Given the specific questions I had, that point may not have even come up in my conversation at the local office.

All I can say is always follow your spirit. No matter what, do what *you* believe God is telling *you* to do. Oh, the best part about the seminar was that it was FREE. A whole day's worth of additional knowledge, and it was absolutely FREE. I love it!

There is a cost to get what you want.
Are you willing to pay the price?

Follow the System

> Do not be deceived, God is not mocked; for
> whatever a man sows, that he will also reap.
> —GALATIANS 6:7 NKJV

I've had a desire for some new clothes; however, it's not as if I can just purchase a brand-new wardrobe at the moment. God reminded me that everything we desire operates on the system of seedtime and harvest. I realized that I probably needed to clean out my closet and give away (sow) some of my garments. It took me a little while to get around to it, but I finally did it.

Next, the task was to place the clothes in someone's possession (put the seed in the ground). I had attempted to give them to my church, but clothing donations were not being accepted at the time. Needless to say, the garments sat in the bag for a while. Then, God told me who I was supposed to give them to. Again, I procrastinated in contacting the lady. I had her email and phone number. I told myself I'd just email her when I was working on the computer or doing the MEDITATION, but I'd always log out or shut down before I reached out to her. Excuses, excuses, excuses…

Check this out. At the ministry where I work, there is a certain person who normally answers the phone on the first or second ring. There's someone else who will usually answer it before I get it. On this particular day, I didn't wait for anyone else; I answered the phone on the first ring. Guess who was on the other end: the lady I was supposed to have contacted. Obviously, I was quite surprised. Of course, she wasn't calling to speak to me, but I explained to her that I had clothes for her ministry that should have been in her possession a while ago. She said she could stop by my workplace and get the clothes out of my car. She picked them up last Friday morning.

Here's the good part. My sister-in-law called me last Friday evening to tell me she had gotten some terrific deals at an outlet near her home. She had purchased a sweater and suede skirt that were regularly over $100 each for only $10 a piece. She had also bought a blouse for around $2. She was calling to obtain my sizes. I was ecstatic when I heard those deals. I told her I'd been saving my money to go shopping, and I desperately needed some business attire. I expressed to her that I would greatly appreciate it if she could select some pieces for me. She and my brother went shopping that evening. When they returned home, my sister-in-law called to inform me they had bought me $127 worth of clothes.

This is the really good part: this sum included two Jones New York suits. Yes, two! I have a total of twelve pieces coming to me for only $127. The other items were name brands also, but I can't even recall the labels right now. All I know is, I have new, quality clothing that was purchased at an exceptional price.

I shared this testimony with you because I could imagine God saying, "Daughter, I'm trying to bless you, but you need to cooperate with My system." He had to actually intervene and put me in a situation where I had no excuse not to sow the clothes. I pray I don't operate in such procrastination again. If God is telling you to sow something, go ahead and do what He told you to do because there is a blessing—a phenomenal blessing—waiting on the other side of your obedience.

Don't take too long to do what He told you to do.

On the Auction Block

And we know that all that happens to us is working for
our good if we love God and are fitting into his plans.
—Romans 8:28 TLB

Finally, I can tell it. As most of you know, we are renting our current home. A few months ago, I spoke with the owner in about a one-minute conversation. She informed me that they needed to sell the house. This news caught me completely off guard because we had almost another year left in our lease.

The owner called again to notify us that the house was about to go into foreclosure. Approximately two weeks later, she phoned to confirm she and her husband were definitely going to lose the house. The home did go into foreclosure, and we were advised it would be auctioned on the steps of the courthouse. Talk about an unimaginable situation.

Everybody around me knew the scripture I was standing on from Psalm 37:25: *I've never seen the righteous forsaken or his seed begging bread.* I can't explain it, but I had total peace during this whole ordeal. I just knew my Father would work everything out for our good. I had no idea how He was going to do it, but I knew He would.

Here's what happened. The house was auctioned and purchased by an investor. I had been in contact with the bank's attorney, inquiring about our rights and various laws surrounding our situation. Because he knew our concerns, he was able to speak highly of us to the purchaser of the house. He even asked the buyer if he would contact us as soon as possible to assure us all was well. Later on in the day of the auction, the purchaser stopped by. All I can say is that we couldn't have had a better person walk through the door.

We were conversing just inside the doorway, so I asked the new homeowner to come in and have a seat. From our conversation, we could tell this gentleman had a very warm and friendly personality. He asked what we had been paying in rent. After we told him, he said we could just continue at that rate. Now, that was truly God because this house could easily rent for more than we're paying. We tried to pay June's rent right there on the spot, but he said we could take care of that later.

We had to pay a security deposit of one month's rent to lease from the previous owners of the home. When we were notified that the house was going into foreclosure and that the owners might file bankruptcy, we wondered if we would ever recover our deposit. After our former landlords received our last rent payment, the wife said she was going to send our rent check back to us. This check was to serve as our security deposit refund. Throughout this entire ordeal, we were able to stay in our home rent free for one month and two days. Praise God! And we have no security deposit under this new rental agreement. You know my God is good! I have to praise and thank Him for being faithful to His Word. And I can say that *I have never seen the righteous forsaken or his seed begging bread!!* Hallelujah.

Hold on to the Word.

Unexpected Increase

> May the Lord give you increase more and
> more, you and your children.
> —Psalm 115:14 NKJV

I can't believe this oversight. I've been neglecting to share God's goodness with you. Two of the most recent happenings involve our vacation and our blessed little man.

Rod and I went on a well-deserved, greatly anticipated cruise vacation. This was our first cruise, and we had a marvelous time. We are already looking forward to our next one. Many of you know we were exercising delayed gratification while getting out of debt, so this was essentially our first real vacation in almost seven years.

I had shared details about our upcoming cruise with my beautician. We planned to get together to go shopping for my trip, but we never had the chance. Anyway, she told me to come by her salon before we left. I stopped by, and she handed me a card and said, "Enjoy your trip!" When I opened the card, $125 was inside along with a note to have a wonderful trip. Don't you know I had a grand time! God is so good. Talk about unexpected income.

The other bit of information I wanted to share concerns my son; we definitely have a blessed child. I am not exaggerating when I say that his *every* need is met. God has moved on the hearts of many people to sow into his life. As I was preparing to share the testimony below, I realized I never shared something that happened last year. Someone on the MEDITATION list requested my address because God had told her to sow a specific seed into Joshua's life. A few days later, we received a letter in the mail. I had to sit down when I saw what was inside. A couple we have never met before sowed a $1,000 seed into our son's life. Yes, you read that correctly—$1,000! I found out later that this young lady and her husband were believing God to conceive, so they were sowing breakthrough seed.

Now, here's what I was originally planning to share. Because the weather is changing, I went into Joshua's room to assess what he needed for the new season. I was pleased to realize God had already taken care of him. A couple we know had given him some clothes a few months back that were too big, so I stored them away. When I pulled those out, I concluded that with those clothes and some other outfits and shoes that had been given to him earlier, he had more than enough—over and above. I will probably have to sow some of the clothes into someone else's life.

Later on, I took a few moments to assess his other needs. He will be 1 ½ on Thursday, and he's been growing quickly. My husband had a carrier in his car that he used whenever I needed him to pick Josh up. It was obvious he needed another car seat.

I mentioned to my husband that Joshua needed a seat. Not even a week later, Rod was talking to the husband of the couple who had given us the clothes, and he said they had a car seat that we could have also. All I could do was thank my Father. As you know, a car seat is not a dollar store investment. Guess what. The car seat that was given to us was actually better than the one Joshua already had in my car. I must say it again: My God is so, so, so, so good!

Always remember and don't ever forget ***GOD IS GOOD!***

My Best Effort

> Take a lesson from the ants, you lazy fellow. Learn
> from their ways and be wise! For though they have
> no king to make them work, yet they labor hard
> all summer, gathering food for the winter.
> —Proverbs 6:6–8 TLB

I was doing some work in my office this past week and began to think about my life, specifically my new business. While meditating on this new venture, I had a truly life-changing experience.

My husband was having some layoffs at his company. Because he's in Human Resources, his company's restructuring has been the topic of conversation around our household. Let me preface what I'm about to share with the fact that I am by no means fearful or worried about my husband losing his job. If you recall, he was laid off from a previous position a while back, and God had His hand all over that situation. This "one-job-income" household lacked nothing. If He did it once, I do believe He can do it again. Thus, my husband being laid off is the least of my concerns.

But back to the story…I was sitting at my desk and these thoughts came to me: *What if he did lose his job? What would I do? How would that change my current actions?* The first answer to emerge pertained to my putting forth more effort into my businesses. As soon as I had that thought, I had a couple more: *Why would you wait until something happened to change your work ethic? If you'd put forth more effort at that time, why not put forth more effort now?* That was a revelation moment for me. I realized how much more

I could be doing to help myself succeed. Because these weren't fear motivated thoughts, I didn't sit and meditate on the negative aspect (my husband losing his job) too long. I immediately took the positive from the thought and determined to do more.

I decided to revisit my prospective customer list to see how many more names I could generate. I made this my project for Friday night and Saturday. Would you believe that after I searched through address books, reviewed list building tools, and thought about people I knew, I came up with an additional 180 plus names? Yes, over 180 names! Now, why didn't I have all those names before? Clearly, I was not putting forth my best effort.

I began to make calls from that list Saturday evening. To date, I have made contact with eight people, two of which are buying a set of diaries each. One of those doesn't even have an upcoming wedding. She's just buying to support my vision. Hallelujah! Four have agreed to forward our website launch email once the site is complete. Another wants to see a sample, so she can spread the word. The last person thought the wedding diaries were a great idea but asked if I was still doing my wake-up calls. She was interested in a birthday greeting for someone and ordering Christmas Greeting calls for her Christmas card list this year. And just think…I have over 170 more calls to make. Is my God good or what!

Bless yourself by doing what you know you need to do.

Signs and Symptoms—Not Facts

> For we walk by faith, not by sight.
> —2 Corinthians 5:7 NKJV

Yesterday, I was not feeling very well. I was tired from not having had the proper rest, and my throat felt as if I were getting a cold. Usually, when I have any sign of a cold, I take something to stop it. The last few times I've taken Theraflu, and it cleared everything up. I mentioned to my husband that I was going to get in the bed early and that I was going to take some Theraflu. He immediately said, "You feel that bad?"

My response was, "No, but I don't want to feel worse."

After I thought about that conversation, I decided not to take the Theraflu. All we had in the house was Severe Cold Theraflu. I considered how silly it would be to take that medicine when I didn't even have a cold. I just *felt* as if I were about to get one. I reasoned how foolish it would be to put that medicine into my body when I didn't even need it. I was just trying to prevent what I *thought* was about to happen.

Another reason I decided not to take the medicine was because I knew I needed to start exercising my faith more. I have to believe God for some substantial things. If I can't believe him to keep me healthy, why even bother with the business matters?

Although I didn't take the medicine, I did get into bed early. Before I went to sleep, I confessed that I was healed and that I will feel totally well in the morning. I declared my healing quite a few times and then dozed off to sleep. As

I write to you this morning, I feel better than I have felt in a very long time. I am well rested and the signs of a cold are gone. I thank God I realized I needed to start trusting Him and not the Theraflu. Don't misunderstand me; I do believe in medicine, but I recognized this was a perfect opportunity to exercise my faith. Again, if I can't believe Him for the little things, how can I expect to receive the big things?

Are you trying to be a Christian without using the Instruction Manual?

He Will Supply

> Casting the whole of your care [all your anxieties, all your worries, all your concerns, once and for all] on Him, for He cares for you affectionately and cares about you watchfully.
> —1 Peter 5:7 amp

One day, I decided to cast my need for a computer entirely on God. It had been a concern of mine, especially with the tasks we had to perform related to Wondrous Works. I knew we would require increased memory, better software, and a more up-to-date computer. I put these necessities in God's hands. I told God that since I knew He had given the vision, He would have to supply the provision. After that day and some thankfulness teaching I received at church, I decided no longer to become frustrated with my computer. I would just thank God when it hung up, when it took forever to load a file, and when the connection to the printer messed up.

Not even a week after I made that decision, Rod was trying to do something on the computer and he asked, "When is Wondrous Works going to get a new computer?" I can't remember exactly how the conversation went, but I think before I even answered, he said he would give $250 toward it. Now, you know I almost passed out. It was as if that comment came out of nowhere. We hadn't discussed the need for a computer recently, and I had not even shared with him my decision to give it to God.

And there's more. I was recently speaking with a friend that I hadn't talked to in a while. We always love to talk about the goodness of our God. Toward the end of the conversation, I was sharing the testimony about the $250. As I was explaining it to her, I had the sense that she was not listening to me or that she was ready to get off the phone; hence, I was just going to end the conversation. She interrupted me and said she wanted to sow toward the computer, too. She commented that she wanted to sow $100. As you'd expect, I was in shock and almost speechless.

In a subsequent conversation, she explained she was quiet because she wanted to make sure she was hearing what God was telling her to do. That, in itself, can be another whole message because I could have been offended if I had not later found out why she wasn't responding the way she normally did to my praise reports. We won't go there right now, though. I believe you can grab that message without any further explanation.

My friend wanted to go ahead and get the check into my hand, so we met this past Saturday. When she handed me the check, I happened to see the amount area did not have "10" at the beginning but "12." She had written the check for $120. I looked at her a bit puzzled. She looked back at me and said something like, "Girl, I know. That was God, honey. I don't know what He's doing, but that's what He told me to write it for. So, I said, 'Okay Lord.'" I hugged and thanked her. She immediately advised me to thank the Lord because it was definitely not her.

In addition to praying for my friend and her family, all I could do on the way home was think of how awesome God is. I meditated on how He really will supply if we will only trust Him to do it. We often get caught up in what we have and what we can do, but God is truly our Source. He will meet every need *if* we allow Him.

Don't depend on yourself; depend on God.

It's All in My Mind

> Don't copy the behavior and customs of this world, but let God transform you into a new person by changing the way you think. Then you will learn to know God's will for you, which is good and pleasing and perfect.
> —ROMANS 12:2 NLT

God is gradually maturing me in several areas. At church, we are being taught on changing our thinking and renewing our mind. I have many areas in which I need to renew my mind, and I've started in some I consider most important—family matters.

Today is another example of how I've applied my change in thinking. My son isn't feeling well, so I had to keep him home from daycare the last two days. Earlier this week, I realized I had much more to accomplish than I thought to be ready for a teleconference with my business partner on Saturday at noon. I had planned to get an earlier than normal start in my day on Thursday and Friday, but as I said, I had to keep Joshua home from daycare, so I was unable to accomplish the many things I had planned.

Instead of being stressed this morning when I realized my son was not going to daycare, I decided to have an entirely new mindset. I recognized God knew I would have to be "mommy" today, so He must have a plan for how I will achieve everything I need to accomplish before tomorrow. Maybe I will have supernatural speed upon me, or I'll get help from somewhere. Perhaps the meeting will be postponed. Obviously, I have no idea what's going to happen. All I do know is that I will complete my outstanding items as long as I trust God. Just making the decision to view this whole situation with that mindset has relieved the stress. I'm sure it will enable me to be a better mommy to Joshua, also.

No matter what you are faced with today, look at it from God's point of view. Remember, He knows everything that is going to happen in our lives. If He allows it to happen, He has already prepared ahead of time a plan to work it out. So, TRUST GOD.

Oh! I have to share this, too. I also realized the most important thing you can do when feeling stressed is spend time with God. Because of all the tasks I needed to accomplish, it would have been quite easy to skip my prayer time and work instead, especially since Josh was asleep. However, I realized I needed to pray. It was during this time that God helped me to see the things I shared above.

UPDATE:

My son slept quite a bit during the day on Friday, so this quiet time allowed me to accomplish part of the items on my To Do list. After Rod arrived home, I was able to complete more work. Then, Saturday morning my partner called to postpone the meeting for an hour and a half. This delay gave me just enough time to finish gathering the last bit of information I needed for our meeting. Didn't I tell you God was going to work everything out? I know one thing: Trusting Him is a much better way to live than being stressed and preoccupied with trying to figure out situations on my own.

When Rod came home, he made a point to tell me that he could "see" the change in me. Now, there's proof for you. Therefore, if you are still struggling with changing your mindset in some area, don't struggle anymore. Just get the Word on it, meditate on that Word, and listen to God's direction. Everything will work out just as He had planned.

Fellowship time with God is vital, not optional.

What Should I Do, God?

Don't act thoughtlessly, but try to find out and
do whatever the Lord wants you to.
—Ephesians 5:17 TLB

I have become much more conscious about how I use my time. I'm trying to make it a habit to ask God what I should do at various times (e.g., morning prayer time) versus just getting into a routine.

Yesterday, while washing my hair, I realized I would have about an hour of stationary time under the dryer. Therefore, I asked God how I should use that time. I was led to a well-known minister's magazine. While reading, I noticed her ministry had believed God for the finances to acquire a new computer system and upgrade some television equipment. As I read further and was becoming more impressed with all the ministry's missions, God told me to send a specific seed to her ministry to assist with obtaining the computer system. When I heard the amount, I told God He would certainly have to confirm that Wondrous Works was supposed to send this seed. It all made sense because, as you know, we believe God for manifestation of our new computer. I needed to make sure, though, especially since it was business money, and I needed to relay this directive to my partner.

As soon as I requested confirmation, I just happened to turn to the verse in the Bible that states, "Whatever you desire that others would do to and for you, even so do also to and for them" (Matthew 7:12 AMP). I believe that was confirmation enough for me. I thought that whole situation was so fascinating. Had I not been sensitive to the leading of the Holy Spirit in how I should spend that time, I may not have given God the opportunity to speak to me. Our business is one of the avenues from which that ministry's seed was to come. I praise God for the opportunity to sow. I also thank Him for the harvest that will return to us—our new computer. Hallelujah!!

Lord, give me instruction for today.
What would you have me do?
What would you have me say?

Rewards of Overcoming the Flesh

> However, let each man of you [without exception] love his wife as [being in a sense] his very own self; and let the wife see that she respects and reverences her husband [that she notices him, regards him, honors him, prefers him, venerates, and esteems him; and that she defers to him, praises him, and loves and admires him exceedingly].
>
> —Ephesians 5:33 AMP

As I shared in a previous MEDITATION, I have been working on improving certain areas of my family life. One of my goals is to better how I relate to, interact with, and treat my spouse. Don't misunderstand me, I'm not some Jezebel, demon-possessed woman, but I knew I could be more to my husband than I was. This was sincerely my heart's desire.

My testimony to you is that God will give you what you need to transform yourself; however, you may be unwilling to receive it. I was ready, willing, and able. I wholeheartedly want to be that virtuous woman I know I can be. God has been ordering my steps, putting me in touch with people I needed to hear, and giving me the tools necessary to succeed.

This past week, I had lunch with a friend who, in the past, has spoken many words of wisdom into my life concerning my responsibilities as a wife. The lunch was supposed to be a casual fellowship time, for we hadn't gotten together in a while. As you may have guessed, it turned into a counseling session. This friend knows me quite intimately. She broke everything down exactly as I needed to hear it, and she directed me on what I should do. Let me tell you, her recommendations were not easy on a sister's flesh. Then again, hearing the truth usually isn't. Nevertheless, I was very willing to receive, and I executed exactly what she instructed.

Because of my decision to listen to her counsel and do what God was telling me to do, Rod and I have a brand-new marriage. Again, by no means were we headed to divorce court; we had a good marriage before I decided to alter my behavior. It's just that our marriage was not at the pinnacle it could have been. The changes I made in myself, the priority I placed on my marriage, and my obedience to God's instructions helped to transform our marriage.

A surprise picnic getaway I planned for my husband also had a significant impact on our relationship. Something happened in the both of us while we were in the park playing a board game that required honest, open communication. Speaking candidly from our hearts, we learned details about each other that we hadn't known in an over 12-year relationship. God is so good!

My point in being so open about our relationship is that God will definitely give you what you desire. However, you must be willing to receive and be obedient, no matter how hard it is on your flesh. One of the actions I had to take as a result of my "counseling session" was to repent to my husband for not being the wife I needed to be for him. It's awesome for me to see how God has changed me over the last seven years of my marriage. Without a doubt, I am not the woman I used to be. Praise God!

Success starts at home.

Do You Have the Guts?

> Behold! I have given you authority and power to trample upon serpents and scorpions, and [physical and mental strength and ability] over all the power that the enemy [possesses]; and nothing shall in any way harm you.
> —LUKE 10:19 AMP

My pastor has been ministering on the believer's authority. Last Wednesday, I wrote the following in my notes: You have the authority. Do you have the guts to use it?

Here's a quick testimony. For a little over a week, my son has been challenged with itching on his posterior. He would be fine all day, but as soon as we removed his clothes at bath time, he'd start scratching. I thought the irritation was allergy related. However, the itching continued, so I took him to the doctor yesterday. She prescribed some creams, and we started applying them last night.

Joshua awoke from sleep very early this morning. He kept whining, tossing, turning, and scratching. He even started scratching his stomach. He seemed to be extremely agitated, much more than normal. Noticing his discomfort, I put him back to bed and stood over him. I knew I needed to exercise my authority as a believer. Ignoring the apprehension I was feeling, I put both my hands on his body and in the name of Jesus commanded whatever it was that was causing the itching and discomfort to leave so that he could rest peacefully. The scratching ceased! I observed him for a few minutes. He did not scratch. He did not toss or turn. He was, in fact, resting peacefully.

I left his room in awe of my Father, thrilled about seeing Him honor His Word. I was grateful that I did not give in to the fear or apprehension but exercised my authority instead. When my pastor preached this message, he did say that exercise breeds confidence. I went into my prayer time with a whole new attitude. I even started talking to the devil and putting him on notice. As we were taught on Wednesday, I took authority over my household and told Satan that neither he nor his cohorts would have any rule in the Pauldin household. I knew God had my back. God has given us authority over every situation and circumstance in our lives.

While I was praying, my son knocked on the door. When I opened it, he had the brightest smile on his face. I couldn't do anything but pick him up and give him a huge squeeze. I kept telling him, "I love you" over and over again. Now, again I say:

> You have the authority.
> Do you have the guts to use it?

Some scripture references from Wednesday:
Luke 10:17–20, Ephesians 6:10, 1 Peter 5:8–9, 1 John 4:4, Matthew 28:18–20, Ephesians 1:18–23, Ephesians 2:1–7, Romans 5:17

*Does your FEAR move you
more than your FAITH?*

Confession Means Protection

> Just as rain and snow descend from the skies and don't go back until they've watered the earth, doing their work of making things grow and blossom, producing seed for farmers and food for the hungry, so will the words that come out of my mouth not come back empty-handed. They'll do the work I sent them to do, they'll complete the assignment I gave them.
> —Isaiah 55:10–11 the message

While driving my son to daycare this morning, I was prompted to say, "I release the angels of God to go before me, my husband, and my son to keep us safe from all hurt, harm, or danger." When I made this confession, it caught my attention because I seldom ever include myself in the confession. I usually just pray for my husband and my son, but this time I had included myself without having made a conscious decision to do so.

I believe I now know why I was prompted to make that declaration. In my attempt to proceed through a yellow light before it turned red, I almost had an accident. A truck was turning in front of me from the lane of oncoming traffic; however, another vehicle was behind it whose driver couldn't see me approaching. As the truck turned, the driver behind it assumed the way was clear and continued to turn along with the truck. I had to slam on brakes and swerve into a lane of what would have been approaching traffic to avoid hitting that car. If some other vehicle had been in the lane into which I swerved, I still would have had a collision.

I have no doubt I was prompted to make that confession earlier this morning to protect me in that situation. Never have I been that close to having an accident. I believe my angels were working to make sure "no hurt, harm, or danger" came nigh to me. Thank you, Lord!!

Speak what He speaks.

Acknowledge Him

> Trust in the Lord with all your heart, and
> lean not on your own understanding;
> In all your ways acknowledge Him, and
> He shall direct your paths.
> —Proverbs 3:5–6 NKJV

During yesterday's service, my pastor stressed how we should acknowledge God in everything we do, especially in these last days. He mentioned we shouldn't do anything just because it seems okay or because we just feel like it. We should acknowledge God concerning the places we go, the restaurants in which we choose to eat, the items we purchase from the grocery store, etc. He stated we need to acknowledge God because the Holy Spirit, who lives on the inside of us, knows all. He knows what is going to happen, when it's going to happen, where it's going to happen, and what has already happened that we may not be aware of.

In recent messages, Pastor has been teaching on being led by the Holy Spirit. The Bible promises He will lead us and show us the right way. He gave us an example from the business world: Just because someone says they'll perform a service for free does not mean we should automatically accept the offer. In some situations, God may have already instructed us regarding who we are to engage for a certain project. Even if that person's price is more than we could have obtained somewhere else, we need to obey God in all situations. Also, that "free" service could easily come with strings attached or an extended time of completion.

I was thinking that our acknowledging God in all our ways even includes the words we choose to say. Just this morning, I made a comment to my husband that I honestly did not mean. It was one of those moments in which my tired flesh was talking. I was able to make amends, but I thought, *If I had acknowledged God before I made that comment—just paused and thought a moment—it wouldn't have been an issue because I'm sure the Holy Spirit would have cautioned me to not say it.* Just something to think about…

*You have a constant companion;
don't ignore Him.*

He Knows Our Needs

Seek the Kingdom of God above all else, and live
righteously, and he will give you everything you need.
—Matthew 6:33 nlt

I must thank God for His goodness. I've been in a state of awe meditating on how God gets us to line up with His plan. Specifically, I'm referring to how I found the new daycare center Joshua is attending. Here's the story.

About a year ago, while in the gym exercising, I overheard a conversation between two women. From what was said, I surmised one woman was a daycare provider. I recognized the other lady because she sang in my church. I didn't know her personally, so she probably didn't even notice me. I heard the daycare provider make a comment about having the kids out in the garden that day. Then she said, "You know I have to share the concept with them." She was referring to seedtime and harvest. When I heard her mention this biblical principal, my interest piqued. I wanted to obtain her information, but for some reason, I wasn't able to do so.

Because the other lady was a member of my church, I figured I'd be able to acquire the provider's name and number from her. For the next several weeks, I looked for the lady who sang in my church every time I attended service. Amazingly, I never saw her again and gradually let the desire to find the provider slip.

Months later, during another visit to the gym, I noticed a childcare facility business card on an information board. I did not know the name of the lady or her facility, but

I thought this could possibly be her. I wrote down the information and later called. I couldn't determine from our brief conversation if this lady was the provider I had been seeking, but once we met (I didn't even remember how she looked), and I started asking questions, I realized she was the lady I had been trying to find all those months ago.

Joshua has been at this lady's center a week and a half, and we have seen tremendous growth. Her center's requirements have not only helped Joshua but us as well. As first-time parents, we don't always know what to do. Even in the times we do know what to do, we sometimes allow our flesh to let things slip. One of this provider's stipulations is that we read to Joshua at least 30 minutes every day. Reading to him at that length was something we were seldom, if ever, doing. Since he's been at her center, we have been diligent in fulfilling our 30-minute minimum. Seeing his progress has actually encouraged us to do more.

When visiting stores now, I catch myself searching for more books and videos. It is amazing to see Joshua develop before my eyes. He has almost memorized some of the books we've been reading him. I just thank God for His awesomeness. He knew exactly what Joshua needed and exactly what we needed. He's a good God!

He will supply exactly what you need.

Untapped Potential

Forget about self-confidence; it's useless.
Cultivate God-confidence.
—1 Corinthians 10:12 the message

You have untapped potential!

I am one to shy away from anything dealing with computer problems. I consider myself to know the basics in Word, Excel, and how to send/receive email. It took me the longest to start using the Internet and let's not even mention PowerPoint. I have allowed fear of the unknown to stop me. Because my husband used to be in the computer field, I usually inform him of any system problems, so he can fix them.

This morning my aversion toward computer problems changed. For the past week, we had been unable to receive messages via email. I was able to send, but every time I tried to receive messages, a certain error notice appeared. Today, I decided I was going to attempt to fix the problem. Can you believe it? It must have been the Holy Spirit because I had this strong desire to resolve the issue. I won't go through many details, but the bottom line is I was able to fix it—with the help of my friend, the Holy Spirit, of course.

This experience provoked me to ponder the fact that we truly do have untapped abilities. I believe fear and our failure to even attempt to solve problems have caused countless missed opportunities.

We were created to do great things. You'll never know what you're capable of until you try. If you are confronted with a challenge today that you normally would not put forth any effort to solve, why not try? You never know what you might discover.

Have a "potential revealing" day!

Take a moment to pray this quick prayer:
Lord, show me things today that I have never seen before.
Now, expect Him to reveal what you've never seen, make plain what you've never understood, and give you ability to do what you've never done.

That Doesn't Belong to Me

> Casting down imaginations, and every high thing that
> exalteth itself against the knowledge of God, and bringing
> into captivity every thought to the obedience of Christ;
> —2 Corinthians 10:5 KJV

A couple of weeks ago, I had an appointment with my gynecologist for an annual exam. Toward the end of the visit, she performed the normal procedures to check my lower abdominal region. The doctor commented that she felt a mass on one of my ovaries. She made a circle the size of a golf ball demonstrating its size. She immediately scheduled an ultrasound.

When I left her office, I was in total shock. All kinds of thoughts started racing through my head. I knew, however, that I had to get control of them and confess what the Word states. After reminding myself of my rights as God's child, I regained my peace. Later that day, I shared the news with my husband. Based on my healing teaching, I said, "I want you to agree with me that I am healed and that all will be well when I go in for the ultrasound to check the mass that the doctor said she felt." That was literally all I said. The next day my husband told me he had prayed about the doctor's report and that I was fine. Outside of those two instances, we mentioned nothing else about the mass.

I'm not going to lie and say that negative thoughts never re-entered my mind again, but, as I said earlier, I took control of them and believed God's Word. I knew in my spirit that all would be well. I wasn't freaking out, stressed out, worried, nothing.

Yesterday, I went in for the ultrasound with total peace. The technician performed all the required tests, and she couldn't find anything. There was no mass. She said everything looked good. Obviously, she had to give a disclaimer that the radiologist had to review the pictures, but I received her report.

While driving away, I meditated on that whole experience from the doctor telling me what she "felt" to my reaction to the waiting period to the technician's report. I recognized that I could have easily let fear come in and give Satan permission to put something on me that wasn't even there in the first place. I realized how important it is to remain calm, stay focused on the Word, and not claim something to be yours that's not. God is good!

Think about what you think about.
Your thoughts just may be
the reason you act the way you act
and feel the way you feel.

A 7-Day Diet

*So we take comfort and are encouraged and confidently
and boldly say, The Lord is my Helper.*
—Hebrews 13:6 amp

My God has done it AGAIN! On Monday and Tuesday of this week, I started calling some of our church prospects to introduce them to the 7-day groom and bride diaries. I secured two meetings for Wednesday and another for next week. Most of the individuals I needed to speak with were not in, so the pursuit will continue today.

As I was preparing for my 11:00 a.m. and 2:30 p.m. appointments yesterday, I was praying in the Spirit and asking God, the Holy Spirit, the angels—EVERYBODY—to help me. As you might guess, I'm a bit uneasy with the sales aspect of the business. Nevertheless, I was going to proceed and do what I knew needed to be done. I was trusting God to lead me, give me the words, and make things happen. This venture into sales definitely required me to exercise my faith.

On the way to my first appointment, I believe God was telling me just to be myself. I had been trying to put on the "salesperson hat" (if there is such a thing), and it was a bit oversized and extremely uncomfortable. To make a long story short…I was totally relaxed, acted like myself, and left there with a sale for 10 SETS of diaries. The sale was not even to the church; it was to the wedding coordinator for the church.

It was clear that God had orchestrated our meeting. When I first spoke to the lady on the phone, she started laughing as soon as I mentioned the names of our products. I wanted to know why she laughed, so I asked shortly after arriving. She confessed that she thought I had said, "7-Day DIET." Now, you do know that if she had allowed me to come into her office thinking I was going to talk about a 7-Day DIET for brides and grooms…that had to be God!

My Father was really working because while I was there, she made a point of showing everyone who entered her office the diaries. It was as if *she* were the salesperson. I guess I was receiving a little on-the-job training from my customer. She also gave me names of people she thought could be potential customers. She even allowed me to display a set of diaries along with some brochures at the church. God is good!

I did not spend as much time at my next appointment, but my Friend showed up at that one as well. I left there with a sale for 4 SETS. Thank you, Jesus!

He doesn't expect you to do it alone.

Something for Joshua

> When Jesus saw what was happening, he was angry
> with his disciples. He said to them, "Let the children
> come to me. Don't stop them! For the Kingdom of
> God belongs to those who are like these children.
> —Mark 10:14 NLT

After returning home from my first day of sales appointments, Rod mentioned my brother had sent me a package. I assumed it was related to business, so I was trying to figure what it could be. I opened the package, and inside was a brand-new business suit and blouse! My brother said it was for my full schedule of meetings with churches. After I put the suit on and looked into the mirror, I was ready to talk to anybody. It's amazing what your attire will do for your confidence. My brother had written a very sweet message to me. He also stated he was sure there was something Joshua needed or wanted, so he included a check for him, too.

Before I reveal the amount of the check, consider this. Joshua had seen a dual electronic basketball game system that he wanted. It cost more than we normally pay for his toys, so my husband jokingly commented, "You better call Grandma." Kidding around, he actually called. Rod told my mom that he was going to teach Joshua faith principles by showing him how to pray and ask God for the game.

I cut the picture out of the sales paper, put it on the refrigerator, and led Joshua in a prayer asking God for the game. I also told him that every time he passed the refrigerator he needed to say, "Thank you, Jesus, for my basketball game." Mr. Joshua constantly reminded us of his desire for the game. He had never been so insistent on anything before. Having had no nudge from us, I would catch him saying, "Thank you, Jesus, for my basketball game."

As God would have it, the check my brother sent Joshua was for $150. The basketball game he desired was $129.99. Talk about ministering to his parents! My husband and I just looked at each other in amazement. We both thought my mother had mentioned something to my brother. I called him to inquire, and he said he had not known anything about the basketball game. This little two-and-a-half year old boy's faith got him his basketball game in less than a week. We told Joshua that Jesus answered his prayer. Uncle Al had sent him a check, and now he could buy his basketball game.

Later that evening, Joshua saw some boxing gloves in a magazine. He said, "Mommy, I want that." Then he said, "Cut it, Mommy. Cut it." He had not forgotten how he was able to acquire the basketball game. I cut out the picture and we prayed. Now, he is eagerly awaiting his boxing gloves.

Dare to believe!
Nothing is going to happen until you believe.

Merry Christmas!

God can do anything, you know—far more than you could
ever imagine or guess or request in your wildest dreams!
—EPHESIANS 3:20 THE MESSAGE

My Father has done it AGAIN! Yesterday, while checking the mail, I noticed a card from our landlords. Because this is the Christmas season, I figured it was the traditional greeting for a happy holiday. I opened the card and read the handwritten note which stated, "Thank you for paying your rent on time and for taking such good care of the house. This is just our way of saying thanks. Enjoy the holidays!"

Inside the card was our $900 December rent check torn in two. Yes, they sent our check back to us torn in two! Did you hear what I said? THEY SENT BACK OUR RENT CHECK!

Now, you know I had to let out quite a few hallelujahs! My son was staring at me as if I had lost my mind. I just told him, "God is good!"

PRAISE GOD! HALLELUJAH! THANK YOU, JESUS!

Be of good cheer!

Whatever

> So I say, let the Holy Spirit guide your lives. Then you
> won't be doing what your sinful nature craves.
> —GALATIANS 5:16 NLT

Our pastors are teaching on controlling our emotions and on hurt. Most of you know whenever a message goes forth you can expect to be tested on it, right? Well, listen to this...

There is a gentleman in my sign language class who used to be the principal at a school for the deaf. He is currently unemployed and has been visiting our class. The teacher often defers to him if she is not 100% sure of a particular hand motion.

During class, our instructor frequently asks if there are any words we would like to know. I had been given a couple different signs for the word *whatever*, so I wanted to know which was correct. I asked the teacher, and she inquired of this gentleman. He said he does not use that word because he thinks it is insulting. We had a brief conversation about how I did not mean it to be insulting, but he was adamant that it was. As you may have guessed, he never did give us the correct sign.

Toward the end of class, I made a comment and this man who never uses *whatever* said, "Whatever" to my comment. The teacher praised him for using *whatever*, and I did too. We were smiling, laughing, and telling him that he did well. I even told him I did not think his expression was insulting. He then remarked to me, "That's because you're not intelligent enough to realize that it was." What! Everything inside me immediately went to boiling point. I think I was in major shock at first; then, I just could not believe he would make such a statement, especially in a room of 12 to 15 people. I think my initial reaction was to throw my hand up (talk to the hand motion) and turn away from him. Even though I was laughing the whole time, I realize now that I probably should not have made that gesture. The class moved on as if nothing had happened. In contrast, I sat there meditating on that insulting comment, and my emotions were doing their own thing.

We always pray at the end of class. This gentleman was about to have surgery, so the teacher was praying for a successful operation. I must be honest and extremely transparent; this sister's heart was not quite there at that moment. Praying for him was the farthest thing from my mind!

While driving home, I kept reflecting on this man's remark. I realized how much words certainly can affect us. I even started doubting and questioning my intelligence. I quickly got those thoughts under control.

This incident was consuming my mind. Wouldn't you know the Holy Spirit stepped right on in. He told me to send this man a card. Now, I was nowhere close to feeling like purchasing him a card, but I knew I had to obey because God had issued the instruction. This man had given me his business card when he first came to class. I looked for it but couldn't find it. I can't say that I was too disappointed about that either.

I did begin to realize, though, that this former principal was probably just angry and hurt. I've heard it said, "Hurt people hurt people." His comment did hurt me. It was, however, the perfect test to see how I would deal with the emotions it sparked.

I eventually found his business card and knew I needed to obey God. By this time, I had my emotions in check and was genuinely trying to bless this man. I had also taken the time to pray the heartfelt prayer for him that I couldn't do in class concerning his surgery, recovery, and overall well-being. I made a point to find just the right greeting card and even included a Pass It On message card with a smiley face wishing good cheer.

The other day *I* received a card in the mail. When I opened it, I was surprised to see it was from this man! He had sent me a card concerning friendship and about how mine inspires, uplifts, blesses, comforts, cheers, renews, encourages, and supports. He was thanking me for being such a wonderful friend. Okay, talk about a total shock. He thanked me for the card and mentioned the surgery was successful. He also shared that he now has to have radiation treatments five days a week for seven or eight weeks.

At the time we were praying for his surgery, I didn't realize his condition was so serious. I thought he was having just a routine operation. However, in one of the subsequent classes the teacher announced he had shared with her that he would have to do radiotherapy. The light bulb came on for me in that class. I realized this man might be dealing with this entire situation all alone. I believe he told me he was also divorced.

In addition to being unemployed, this man was probably facing the toughest health challenge of his life. I believe he simply needed someone to reach out to him, especially if he was calling me a "friend."

I'm sure you understand how much this experience tested me. I wanted to be detailed in my explanation of this test so you could realize you don't always need to fly off the handle and *react* instead of *respond*. There's always a reason behind a person's behavior. I am so thankful that I was able to hear God throughout this whole situation and be obedient to his instructions. I believe that man will cherish the card and may even take that Pass It On smiley face with him while he's having his radiation treatments.

Thank God for the fruit of the Spirit.

God has an unlimited supply of grace and mercy. What about you? You're made in His image. How's your supply?

Thinking Outside the Box

> Let those who favor my righteous cause and have pleasure in my uprightness shout for joy and be glad and say continually, Let the Lord be magnified, Who takes pleasure in the prosperity of His servant.
> —PSALM 35:27 AMP

On March 16, I sent the following MEDITATION:

Be creative…make your own way prosperous!

Many times we are seeking God for answers and direction, but we don't open our minds to other options or possibilities. The thing you desire may be in YOUR ABILITY TO CREATE. If there is an "ideal" situation you desire, there may very well be a way for you to have it. It just may require your thinking outside the box. Be creative…make your own way prosperous.

You know there's a story behind this, right? Look forward to it. ☺

Now, for today's MEDITATION…

The story begins with me trying to find a part-time job. I needed something very flexible and close to home. I faced challenges working during the day as well as the evening. Because my husband is the primary income earner in the family and works a considerable distance from home, I am responsible for picking up Joshua from school and staying home with him if he's not well. I didn't believe a part-time employer would approve my leaving work to care for my child. Then, when I considered working evenings, I knew Rod had to travel sometimes, so I would need to be home with Josh those evenings. In addition to that, I had to have time to work on my businesses.

These challenges were of great concern because I finally felt it was okay to find a job. During one period, I honestly believed God did not want me to work. Now that I had a release to do so, I was facing all these obstacles. An employment opportunity was presented to me, but I knew it was not what I was supposed to do. The opportunity did, however, jump-start my brain to begin thinking outside the box.

I eventually had this Holy Spirit idea to submit a proposal to a former employer to do some much needed accounting work in an independent contractor capacity. Please note I had never seen a proposal, much less written one. I believed this idea was from God though, so I knew He would help me compose it. I did some research, drafted and redrafted the proposal, and finally submitted it for consideration.

I met with the chief executive officer of the company last week. My proposal was APPROVED. The CEO had nothing but praises related to the document. Words such as "excellent" and "very impressed" were repeated constantly throughout our meeting. She expressed that she knew I had invested a lot of time and thought into preparing the proposal. She had even highlighted certain phrases and sentences she was most impressed with. The meeting went exceptionally well. I will start the project on April 11.

Clearly, offering my services to this company was a God idea. Working as an independent contractor will allow me to set my own schedule and have the necessary flexibility I desire. I had not even thought about contracting. All I was considering was a traditional j-o-b. I honestly was not even entertaining accounting too much because I knew how demanding it could be. This work arrangement proves God really will give us the desires of our heart. We need only be open to allowing Him to work any way He chooses.

So I repeat, the thing you desire may be in YOUR ABILITY TO CREATE. If there is an "ideal" situation you desire, there may very well be a way for you to have it. It just may require your thinking outside the box. Be creative…make your own way prosperous!

*You can accomplish your goal.
You may not know the specific steps
just yet, but it can be done!*

Honor Breeds Honor

Anyone who wants to be my disciple must follow
me, because my servants must be where I am. And
the Father will honor anyone who serves me.
—JOHN 12:26 NLT

My God has done it AGAIN! While checking my email yesterday, I read a message that confirmed how extraordinary God is. Someone on the MEDITATION distribution list had sent me a message that left me speechless.

This young lady has a folder in her email where she keeps some of my meditations. She said she refers to them at times, and yesterday was one of those times. She went on to say that a particular MEDITATION blessed her all over again. She added that she loves my spirit and everything I stand for. Her words were truly heartwarming. I love to hear how God is using me to bless others. As you know, I give Him all the glory for what He brings forth in the meditations.

Here is what astounded me. She has decided she wants to sow a regular seed into my personal life. She made it clear that it was just for me—"for your hair, nails, clothing, car cleaning, meals, etc…whatever you want to use it for." Now, you know I almost passed out when I read those words. God is so good! This blessing was just so timely.

A couple months ago, a minister came to our church and spoke on honoring God. He did a thorough teaching on honor, too much for me to share here. Basically, he explained our honor for God is truly demonstrated in the financial seeds we give to Him. He said there is no honor without substance, and one way we honor God is to honor our man and woman of God. He also stated, "Honor contains an uncomfortable amount of money."

After his series of messages, I decided I wanted to act on the word and "honor" God. My husband and I have established allowances we give ourselves each time he gets paid. This is all the money we have to use as our own. It has to buy anything we want, be it lunch, personal care, what-nots, etc. This allowance is our personal spending money, and once it's gone, it's gone. We allot the same amount twice a month. I decided I was going to start sowing my end-of-month allowance. I knew that amount would definitely be an uncomfortable sum because I would essentially have no spending money for two weeks. In addition, God had already allocated part of my mid-month allowance, so allocating my end-of-month allowance was certainly going to cost me.

I gave my first seed in March and recently gave the second at the end of April. It was also at the end of April that I gave the seed from my first paycheck. I must admit the thought did pop up to possibly skip this month, for I was giving such a large seed anyway. I knew that was not God, so I quickly dismissed the thought, never considered it again, and gladly gave my allowance.

When I made the decision to sow my honor seed, I realized I would have to trust God to supply my needs. I was certain He would. I had no idea how, but I knew if I honored Him, He would honor me. Now, you can understand why that email message was so significant. When I first read it, I just sat in awe, but a few minutes later, the Holy Spirit reminded me of the seeds (my allowance) that I had sown. It was almost as if He was telling me, "See, I told you I would supply your needs."

I thank God for where He is taking me in Him. We have to learn to TRUST GOD and in Him alone. We cannot put our faith in man, our spouses, our paychecks, or anything else. Our hope must be in God. He has set up the system, and if we work it, I believe we can have the abundant life He promised!!

Is your servanthood authentic?

Out of the Mouth of Babes

Children are a gift from God; they are his reward.
—Psalm 127:3 TLB

After I picked Joshua up from school yesterday, I had to run some errands. At around 6:33 p.m. and totally out of the blue, my son (now 3) asked, "Mommy, are we going to church?" I was surprised by his question, especially since I had decided we would not attend that evening. A few moments of silence passed before I answered. Then, I believe I asked him if he wanted to go, and he replied, "Yes." To my knowledge, Joshua has never asked us that question, and I had not mentioned anything about that day being the day we go to church.

After a couple minutes of overcoming the flesh and realizing that inquiry was probably God speaking through my son, I decided we were going. On a normal Wednesday, we leave for church around 6:20 p.m., and we've already eaten. It was past 6:20, and I had not fed Joshua. Nonetheless, I knew I needed to be there, so we ate in the car on the way to church.

As you might guess, the message my pastor preached was exactly what I needed. His title was "The Anatomy of Success." I won't even try to repeat it, but I was focused on every word coming out of his mouth. It seemed as if he touched on a little of everything I was dealing with. I was thrilled I had listened to my son. As we were riding home, I thanked Joshua for asking me if we were going to church.

God is faithful to make sure we're in the right place at the right time. He knows I'm working on certain areas and trying to make some necessary changes in my life. He showed me exactly how to get that done last night. GOD IS AWESOME!

*God's voice can sound exactly
like someone else you know.*

A Few Butterflies, But Pressing On

> Behold, I am doing a new thing! Now it springs
> forth; do you not perceive and know it and will
> you not give heed to it? I will even make a way
> in the wilderness and rivers in the desert.
> —Isaiah 43:19 AMP

Rod and I had been searching for a new home for a while. We put a contract on one a little over a month ago and here's what happened.

The house came on the market late one night. Our agent recognized the neighborhood. She knew the price was ridiculously low, so she called to make an appointment. I was the first to see the home the next morning and couldn't believe the condition. It was well-maintained and appeared to have nothing wrong with it. Besides not being a ranch, this house had everything we wanted. Without having seen the home, my husband agreed to make an offer.

By the end of the day, three other offers had been submitted, so all of us were asked to resubmit new bids. Rod and I were in a very precarious situation and had only about an hour to decide on our new offer. We won the bid, but we were both uncertain about our decision.

I was a serious wreck the next day. I was so distracted that I couldn't do anything requiring focus. I kept petitioning God for help. There was no way I could go another 30 days until closing in this condition. I needed Him to speak to me and tell me something, one way or the other. The decision had even affected my sleep.

After a day of total consumption over whether we had made the right choice, it was time to retire. Once in bed, I remembered I had not read the scriptures from the Daily Bible Reading Plan we are using this year. My first reaction was to read it the next day; however, the Holy Spirit would not let me rest. I got up to read the text for that day. The Word that I needed to regain my peace was in that day's passage…Psalm 55:22: *Cast your burden on the Lord [releasing the weight of it] and He will sustain you; He will never allow the [consistently] righteous to be moved (made to slip, fall, or fail).*

All I could do was smile and thank God. You don't understand how much I needed that scripture. Afterwards, I just held on to that Word knowing that no matter what, God was going to take care of us. He would not allow us to slip, fall, or fail. I knew that even if we hadn't made the right decision, He would not allow us to fail.

Moving things on a bit…We were set to close this past Tuesday. I reminded my husband to make sure he obtained the paperwork, so he could read it before we went to the close. He met with the mortgage broker Monday afternoon and much to our surprise the interest rate on our loan had gone up 1.25%. This caused our monthly payment to go up almost $200.

My husband and I discussed the rate change that evening and decided to cancel the purchase. The next morning, the day of the scheduled closing, the mortgage broker called to make us an offer. Rod and I went to breakfast, discussed it, and decided we did not need to proceed. We called the broker back and informed him the deal was still off. While we were on the phone, another offer was made. We got off the phone, prayed, discussed it, and decided to accept the offer. At this point, the closing was only about an hour and a half away.

I'm almost finished (I promise), but I have to share this last part. A couple of people at work knew we had closed on the house, so they asked whether I was excited. To be honest, the mixed feelings remained because I was still questioning whether this house was God's will. I wanted to be 100% sure of our decision, and I genuinely wasn't. After I left work, I was driving down the road considering why I was not able to rejoice like the average new homeowner would.

On the way home, I had to stop by the post office. I walked up to the door and a gentleman said, "Let me get that for you." I thanked him and proceeded to check my box. I was about to go back out the door when the same gentleman said, "Ma'am, let me get that for you."

I said, "Thank you very much!"

He commented, "That's how you get your blessings."

I replied, "I know that's right."

Then, as I turned to head toward my car, the same gentleman said, "You keep that faith up. You've come too far to turn back now." Then, he said, "Be blessed," and got into his truck.

I smiled from ear to ear and said, "I receive that."

I got in my car knowing that God had just allowed that dialogue so I would know we were on the right track. I immediately became joyful about our new home! I received that man's words as my confirmation.

I must admit I still have a few butterflies because we have much more house than we set out to purchase, yet I now believe God is just taking us to a new level. Wow, I literally just realized our new house is almost exactly double the square footage we're living in now; it's actually four square feet more. To God be the glory!

Just so you know, I'm working on something else too. Stay tuned...

No matter what the situation looks like, seems like, or feels like, stay in His will.

Faithful Family Members

> May God prosper you and your family and
> multiply everything you own.
> —1 Samuel 25:6 TLB

The closing on our house was September 20. We had not planned to move until October 1, so I figured we would have enough time to clean and prepare the house to our liking. My parents had offered to help clean because they couldn't come the weekend of the move. I assured them I would be fine, and they didn't need to make a special trip.

THANK GOD THEY DIDN'T LISTEN! They and my mother- and sister-in-law came from North Carolina to help us. We worked for two full days, and there were still tasks to be done after they left. My family worked eleven or twelve hours each day. This sista is wholeheartedly grateful! There is no way I could have cleaned that entire house the way I wanted by the first of the month. In addition, the men took care of some painting that needed to be done. Praise God for hardworking family members. They even pitched in when things needed to be purchased. GOD IS GOOD!

Of course, certain people, who will remain nameless, wanted to know which room belonged to them. I had told them they would have to share a space with Josh's toys because Makenzie would need a room once she manifests. Later, my husband said the nursery could be combined with Josh's playroom; therefore, they could have the other bedroom. They were elated to hear this news. To ensure they had somewhere to sleep when they visited, they purchased a bedroom set and are in the process of decorating the room. PRAISE GOD for some furniture! When we decided to buy this house, I told Rod we needed to sow seed for furniture because the Lord will have to furnish it. I guess the seed is working!

Oh, I couldn't forget this…we've also received a $1,000 "housewarming" gift. PRAISE JESUS! THANK YOU, LORD!

I should probably close now and start creating some order around here. Boxes, boxes, boxes, everywhere…

Goodness. Goodness. Goodness.
Thank God for His goodness!

Do It Afraid

> But Jesus ignored their comments and said to
> Jairus, "Don't be afraid. Just trust me."
> —Mark 5:36 TLB

I shared in the MEDITATION concerning the purchase of our home that I was working on something else. The something else has manifested, and I am excited to share…

WE BOUGHT ANOTHER HOUSE! Can you believe it? Two houses in less than 50 days. Talk about stepping out in faith!

Yes, there is a story behind this, so let's get to it. As you know, we were renting our previous residence before we purchased our current home. After receiving some training in real estate investing, I started throwing around the idea of our purchasing that home as an investment. Rod was not in agreement because of the problems he felt existed with the house. I knew the "problems" were all cosmetic, so I kept trying to convince him that those things didn't matter for a rental.

After we purchased our current home, and my eyes were opened even more to the awesome opportunities in real estate, I resumed my talks about the rental purchase. My husband kept asking what I was going to do. I had a bit of fear creep in concerning the whole idea. From asking our previous landlords if we could buy the house for a price less than I figured they would want (I'm not the bold negotiator type) to realizing this would be a giant leap into a whole new area in which I had no experience, the anxiety was definitely present.

I put off calling our previous landlords as long as I could. Then, one day I believe the Holy Spirit was prompting me to make the phone call at that particular time. I called to put the offer on the table. They had offered to sell us the house from the time they bought it in foreclosure, but we had not been interested. Additionally, the price was higher than we wanted to pay. The fear was present because I was willing to pay only $100,000 for the house. I knew it was worth more, so I had thoughts going through my mind of them totally dismissing the idea and thinking I was completely clueless. The day that I felt I was supposed to call, I just kept saying to myself, "All they can say is 'Yes' or 'No.'" I had to talk myself into making that phone call. You can't imagine how nervous I was.

By the end of the conversation, our previous landlords accepted the offer. I was ecstatic, especially because Rod had basically separated himself from the whole deal and put the decision on me. He said that if I wanted it, I could get it. In conversations, he kept referring to it as *my* house. I had even mentioned it to someone else in my family, and he commented he didn't think the house was worth $100,000. All that didn't even matter to me. I just knew I was supposed to pursue this purchase, and I also knew that the appraisal would tell the true worth anyway.

After I got off the phone from hearing their acceptance, I ran outside to tell my husband the news. He was genuinely happy for me. I was thrilled and felt a great sense of accomplishment. This experience also allowed me to see how fear can stop us from getting what God has for us.

Jumping ahead a little, the house appraised for $120,000. Now, for a first property, I do believe I did a mighty fine job! Having an investment in real estate is unquestionably new territory, though. I was at the property last week doing some painting. I have never painted a room in my life. I told the Lord He would have to help me. I must say we (the Holy Spirit and I) did a mighty fine job on that, too. Because I was not working, I was there during the day. My husband came over in the evenings. It was fascinating to see how intrigued he appeared as he examined my work; he couldn't find anything wrong. He was quite impressed.

In addition to securing such a great deal on the house, we have much favor with our previous landlords. The wife has given me an open door to use her tenant application, rental agreement, and other paperwork as well as a list of their repairmen. The husband came over while I was painting and explained how I could fix things without spending much money. He even said I should check with him before I buy any tools because he already has most of the things we need. In addition, he offered us his pressure washer to clean the outside of the house and the deck. He also said that because we live about 15 miles away, he could act as my property manager and show the house for me. They literally live right around the corner. He added he would be more than happy to do that for me! Talk about the FAVOR of GOD!

The official closing was yesterday, so you know I had to tell of His goodness today. By the way, someone is quite involved with the whole process now. We are working on getting *our* house prepared for renters. I knew he would come around, especially since he had to sign his name on the dotted line yesterday to buy it. Thanks, honey!

Don't allow fear to keep you from your destiny.

Act Like It's So

> And when he was brought to his mother, he sat
> on her knees till noon, and then died.
> And she went up and laid him on the bed of the man
> of God, and shut the door upon him and went out.
> And she called to her husband and said, Send me one
> of the servants and one of the donkeys, that I may go
> quickly to the man of God and come back again.
> And he said, Why go to him today? It is neither the New
> Moon nor the Sabbath. And she said, It will be all right.
> Then she saddled the donkey and said to her servant, Ride
> fast; do not slacken your pace for me unless I tell you.
> So she set out and came to the man of God at Mount
> Carmel. When the man of God saw her afar off, he said to
> Gehazi his servant, Behold, yonder is that Shunammite.
> Run to meet her and say, Is it well with you? Well with your
> husband? Well with the child? And she answered, It is well.
> —2 KINGS 4:20–26 AMP

I've mentioned my husband and I believe God to conceive again. We've actually been talking about our new addition to the family around the house. Joshua keeps asking when his little sister will be here. I explained to him that he's going to get one, but she's not here yet. I told him she's in heaven with God. Well, Mr. Joshua sincerely believes he has a sister. He is even telling other people about her.

While we were home for Thanksgiving, one morning Joshua got up before I did. He joined some other family members in the great room. As they interacted with him, Joshua informed them that he has a baby sister, and she is in his mommy's stomach. As soon as I walked into the room, all eyes turned to me. Of course, they instantly asked if there was something I needed to share.

When I picked Josh up from school on Friday, he had announced to the teacher's assistant that he had a baby sister as well. She asked me about it, and I clarified by explaining we are operating in faith right now. She stated Joshua was certainly spreading the word for us.

Just the other day I was ironing some clothes and laid them across the crib. With a bit of frustration, Joshua immediately asked me why I was putting my clothes on his sister's bed...Alrighty then!

I keep dwelling on how Joshua genuinely believes he has a sister and how he is telling everyone about her. Is that not what we are supposed to do? I have to remind myself constantly that FAITH SPEAKS and FAITH IS NOW. Faith is always in the present tense. My son is definitely teaching me a lesson. I told Rod we need to get with the program.

It doesn't matter what the circumstance looks like.

A True Christ-like One

> Therefore be imitators of God [copy Him and follow His example], as well-beloved children [imitate their father].
> —Ephesians 5:1 AMP

We have a quarterly pest control contract, and the technician serviced our house yesterday. He was an older Hispanic gentleman with a friendly demeanor and terrific attitude.

Almost as soon as he walked through the door, I discerned there was something different about him. In our conversation, he mentioned he was a Christian so that led into further discussion. I sincerely enjoyed speaking with him because I perceived he was very genuine. What impressed me most was his positive attitude. Every statement he made was hopeful and uplifting.

After he performed his job, which was done professionally and with excellence, all I could think about was how perfect an example he displayed of what a "Christ-like" person should be. Therefore, I have a few questions for you:

- What impression are you leaving on those with whom you come into contact?
- Do they think they've just interacted with a saint or a sinner?
- Are they glad you're gone or wish you could have stayed?

Act like your Father.

Exceeding Abundantly Above

> He [God] Himself has said, I will not in any way fail you nor give you up nor leave you without support. [I will] not, [I will] not, [I will] not in any degree leave you helpless nor forsake nor let [you] down (relax My hold on you)! [Assuredly not!]
> —Hebrews 13:5 AMP

A couple months ago I decided I needed to find a part-time job. I consistently searched the paper and made inquiries but didn't find anything of interest. I did notice a few jobs, but from my perspective, the benefit did not outweigh the costs. I also found an accounting ad for this side of town that required Peachtree Accounting software experience. It appeared to be the perfect fit. I submitted my résumé but never heard a word.

There was still hope, though. A gentleman for whom I had done some contract work asked if I would be interested in working for a client I had previously helped him with. They had requested his services, but he explained his rate would be higher if they used my skills through his company. This organization had been a long-time client, so he advised them they were welcome to speak with me directly, thereby cutting him out of the deal.

I had the interview last Tuesday. It didn't even have the semblance of an interview, though. I had been referred with such high praises that I believe the decision had already been made. The only items we had to agree on were my rate and hours. They wanted me to work 8 to 5, but that didn't quite line up with my vision. We had to negotiate just a bit. The gentleman I met with stated he had to obtain approval for my rate, and I'd hear from him by Friday. He called early Wednesday morning. He cheerfully advised he'd see me Monday morning to get started.

The best part about all this is that I will be making almost double what I had decided I wanted my minimum hourly wage to be. God is an over-the-top God! He never ceases to amaze me! I kept reminding Him of my current commitments and future desires. I had to cast down thoughts that I just needed to find something—anything—because my time was running out. Deep down, I knew that wasn't my God…I was sure He'd have something especially for me.

God has some wonderful surprises for you!

Scrumptious Strawberries

> The thief comes only in order to steal and kill and destroy. I came that they may have and enjoy life, and have it in abundance (to the full, till it overflows).
> —John 10:10 AMP

After I picked my son up from school Wednesday evening, out of the blue he announced he wanted strawberries. I repeated what he said to make sure he was serious. Then, I told him we'd stop and buy some. Frankly, I don't normally purchase strawberries, and when Joshua makes requests, I usually say I'll get it when I go grocery shopping. But this day was different.

He was so excited about purchasing these strawberries. He joyfully held them in his lap all the way home. Once we were inside the house, he immediately asked if he could wash them. Josh stepped up on his stool, and I rolled up his sleeves. He stood there looking as if he belonged in the kitchen. (His dad lets him cook with him sometimes.)

As he sat eating the strawberries with this expression of pure bliss on his face, all I could think about was how happy he was simply to be sitting there eating strawberries. In between all his smacking, he even said to me, "Mmmm, this is good."

It gave me such joy to know that I had bought these for him. There was a time in my life when I would not have purchased strawberries just because I thought they were too expensive, especially this time of year. Thankfully, I'm starting to see things in a whole new light.

Just yesterday, an older gentleman I work with had some

dessert catalogs at his desk. I asked if he orders from them. He said he did, and he proceeded to show me what he purchases. As he was pointing to the items, he commented, "You know we have to enjoy our lives." This statement is so true.

I believe we get so caught up in the busyness of our lives that we sometimes forget to ENJOY LIFE. Consider the immense amount of pleasure a simple carton of strawberries brought to this little boy…priceless!

Take time to smell the roses. The smallest thing can bring the greatest joy.

Yay! We Have Tenants!

*We're not keeping this quiet, not on your life.
Just like the psalmist who wrote, "I believed
it, so I said it," we say what we believe.*
—2 Corinthians 4:13 the message

You've probably heard a minister exclaim, "Praise Him as if you already have it" or instruct you to "Act like it's so." Here is something that had an extreme impact on me related to our "acting like it's so."

When my husband arrived home from working at our rental property, he was speaking faith when he made a comment about our "new tenants." I added another comment remaining consistent with his faith-filled words. Then, my son jumped in and started bouncing up and down in his seat with both arms raised high in the air yelling, "Yay! We have tenants! We have tenants!" He was smiling from ear to ear. His face had all the joy I realized my face should have displayed if I had just received word that we truly did have tenants.

After that incident, I could not dismiss the lesson. So, this is merely a checkup message. Are you really acting as if it's so? Are you thanking Him as if it has already happened? Are you speaking in line with what you say you believe?

By the way, confession does work. Yay! We have tenants! We have tenants!

What you say is what you get.

Promotion in the House

> Beloved, I pray that you may prosper in all things
> and be in health, just as your soul prospers.
> —3 John 2 NKJV

MY GOD HAS DONE IT ONCE AGAIN! In the MEDITATION on favor from July 22, I wrote, "I want to let you know that God is raising up somebody, somewhere who will use their power, ability, and influence to help me get my new home, two reliable vehicles, growth in my businesses, and my husband to receive promotion on his job."

As you are aware, we moved into our new home October 1. In addition, the vehicles we currently drive are now reliable (at the writing above, something was wrong with mine, but no one could figure out the problem). I'm still working on the growth in the businesses area. (Hmmm, that may be the problem—"I" am still working on the growth.) But the last one is now a reality. My husband has received his promotion.

There was a new position which was to become available at my husband's current company. The person responsible for hiring someone for the job approached Rod and asked if he would be interested. After thinking it over, he accepted the offer. She later showed him the salary she had budgeted for the position.

Everything I just shared happened prior to purchasing our new home. While we were looking, my husband kept moving outside of our agreed price range. As you'd expect, changing our price range based on a promised salary was quite disturbing to me. My thought process is that anybody can promise you anything, especially in corporate America, but that doesn't mean it's going to happen. Therefore, I definitely did not want to purchase a home based on a potential future salary.

Obviously, I eventually gained my peace concerning the whole situation, and we moved forward with the purchase. I must admit this was the biggest leap of faith I've ever taken. Once I had peace about proceeding, I began to focus on the fact that God is our Source. I reasoned that if He gave us peace to move forward, He obviously would supply our every need.

As I've shared, God has increased me since we've been in the house, and now he has increased my husband. Effective January 16, he will be promoted to an HR Manager. This position increases his base salary almost 17%. Yes, you read that figure correctly, seventeen percent! And you know God is a God of exceeding abundantly above. He will now also be eligible for bonuses.

God is incomparable. No words can describe His faithfulness. If you allow Him to direct your steps, get outside your comfort zone, and overcome the fear, I believe He will do more than you ever dreamed.

He is faithful. He will do it.

The $50 Shoes

And I will ask the Father, and He will give
you another Comforter (Counselor, Helper,
Intercessor, Advocate, Strengthener, and Standby),
that He may remain with you forever.
—JOHN 14:16 AMP

I had another lesson in parenting and following the prompting of the Holy Spirit yesterday. I must share…

Joshua was in serious need of new shoes for school. He wears a uniform each day which includes vest and tie. His worn-out shoes were not complimenting his uniform at all. We had searched for shoes but couldn't find any we liked. As a last resort, I went to Stride Rite. Now, anyone who is a patron knows their shoes are costly for us frugal shoppers. When I turned over the shoe I liked and noticed the price, I was immediately reminded I was not in Walmart. I decided to bite the bullet and purchase the $50 shoes. Just so you know, I don't even pay $50 for my own shoes. (Love DSW's clearance racks!)

I kept thinking I should probably explain to Joshua that he needs to be careful in these shoes, but I never said anything to him. I guess I almost thought it was pointless. My husband often tells me that I talk to him above his level sometimes. Of course, I don't think so because he always seems to understand when I do share certain things with him.

Well, yesterday when I picked him up (only the fourth day of wearing his $50 shoes) much to my dismay, he had major scuffs on the front of his shoes. After I asked how it happened, he joyfully proceeded to tell me how he had used his shoes to stop his swing on the playground. The swings are on cement! I couldn't believe it. I began to point out to him that that was not a good thing to do. I explained those shoes cost too much for him to mess them up like that. Would you like to know the first words he spoke to me? He said, "Mommy, you have to tell me if I'm not supposed to mess them up." I couldn't say a word because I knew the Holy Spirit had prompted me to tell him, but I didn't act.

All I can say is this: There's no better lesson than one that comes with a price tag. You'd better believe I won't make that mistake again!

Listen to your spirit.

Unfinished and Underdeveloped

> In view of all this, make every effort to respond to God's promises. Supplement your faith with a generous provision of moral excellence, and moral excellence with knowledge, and knowledge with self-control, and self-control with patient endurance, and patient endurance with godliness, and godliness with brotherly affection, and brotherly affection with love for everyone. The more you grow like this, the more productive and useful you will be in your knowledge of our Lord Jesus Christ.
> —2 Peter 1:5–8 nlt

While reviewing some of my old notes from church, I came across the following: "I have the potential. I've just been living underdeveloped."

I immediately had the image of a building under construction but at a standstill. I thought of what I would think as I passed by that building every day. One question which would come to mind is "When are they ever going to finish it?"

This subject of being unfinished is particularly relevant to me right now because our homeowners association has asked if they can construct a subdivision sign on a portion of our property. I had a little hesitation because I know the history of the sign at the other entrance. In my opinion, it took much too long to complete. I was just speaking with my neighbor about how much it would irritate me to see this unfinished sign staring me in the face every time I drive up to my house.

Another thought came to mind right after the vision of the building. I realized that "irritated" is probably exactly how God feels about me. He has placed His potential on the inside of me, but I have only been existing, like that building and that sign—underdeveloped. Inside me is everything I need to accomplish all the good things He has planned for my life, but I keep allowing year after year after year to pass by. I have not made it a priority to develop what God has started in me. Because I am referring to God, I guess *saddened* or *displeased* may be better words than "irritated." *Irritated* seems a bit harsh for a loving Father. I'm sure you get the picture, though.

Don't you think it's time for you to discover what God meant for you to be?

Are you in a holding pattern?

Slam on Brakes and Pray

> As for God, His way is perfect! The word of the
> Lord is tested and tried; He is a shield to all those
> who take refuge and put their trust in Him.
> —Psalm 18:30 AMP

You know you're genuinely saved when you see a change in your responses to certain happenings in the course of a normal day…

I was on the way home from taking Josh to school, and the driver of a truck pulled out in front of me. To be clear, he literally drove onto the road just a few feet away from my 45 mph oncoming vehicle. I was almost directly in front of him and had to slam on brakes to avoid hitting him. I believe that's the closest anyone has ever come and not had a wreck.

Right after he pulled out, I didn't say a word or show any outward signs of disgust or lay on my horn. While staring at the back of his slow-moving truck, I simply reclined against my seat with an expression of absolute confusion on my face. I was in shock over what he had done, primarily because I was approaching so fast. After I overcame the shock, I noticed he kept looking back at me. He probably thought I was going to throw up a finger or something. I just smiled and said, "Lord, bless him."

As a result of this event, I considered how easily I could have let it bother me or even send me into a rage. But, as I mentioned, I just smiled, went another couple miles down the highway, and turned onto my road, not bothered at all by what had just happened. It's amazing how our responses change when we allow God's way to rule.

God is good to all, so you should be good to all.

I'm Only a Vessel

Listen, son of mine, to what I say. Listen carefully. Keep these thoughts ever in mind; let them penetrate deep within your heart.
—Proverbs 4:20–21 TLB

Someone on the MEDITATION distribution list sent me one of my meditations in response to yesterday's message. Once I read it, I realized more than ever that I am just an instrument God uses to relay what He wants communicated. I often forget that I need to reread and reflect on many of the messages as well.

I was actually reminded of a couple ministers I frequently listen to and how they often say they feed off their own messages. I had never made that connection before because I, of course, have never seen myself or the meditations in the same light as a message from a man or woman of God. However, I suppose in reference to hearing what God has to say, this comparison is valid. I have always professed that what comes forth is not me, and God gets all the glory. I guess I never realized how important it is for *me* to really *listen* to what I say, no what He says through me. That is, I need to listen for more than just one day.

If you're in a position where God is often using you to minister to others, don't forget to listen to your own words and earnestly consider what you're saying. I know for a fact many of the messages God has me share are for me, too. Sometimes, I feel as if they're especially for me!

Pay attention.

About the Author

From her childhood till now, Shawanda Pauldin's aspiration has been to please God and be in His perfect will. A homemaker for many years, Shawanda spent a vast amount of time volunteering at her church and a local outreach ministry. Over the years, she has worked in corporate America, operated her own businesses, and held various contract positions.

By nature, Shawanda has an energetic personality and an inspirational spirit. She loves to uplift others by speaking words of truth and hope. Her life is an open book. Anytime she can testify about a life experience or share a word of encouragement, she's eager to do so. Her greatest asset is her contagious spirit.

Unquestionably, her most cherished roles are wife and mother. Married more than 17 years, she and her husband have enjoyed an over 21-year relationship as best friends. In recent years, Shawanda obeyed God's call on her life to homeschool her children. She resides in metropolitan Atlanta with her husband and two sons. For more information or to contact Shawanda, visit www.WWinspires.com.